This Coloring Book

Belongs: _______________

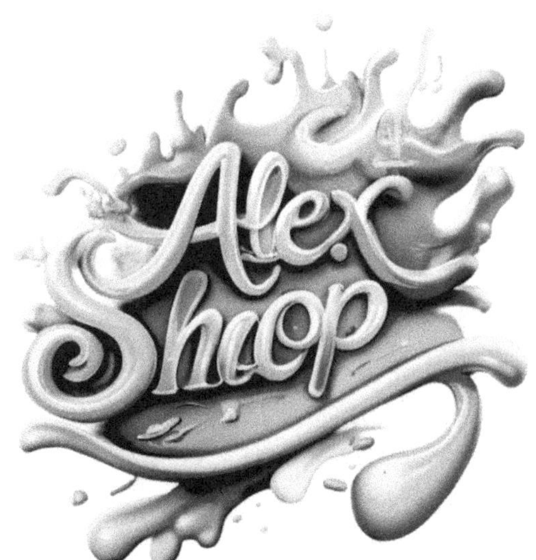

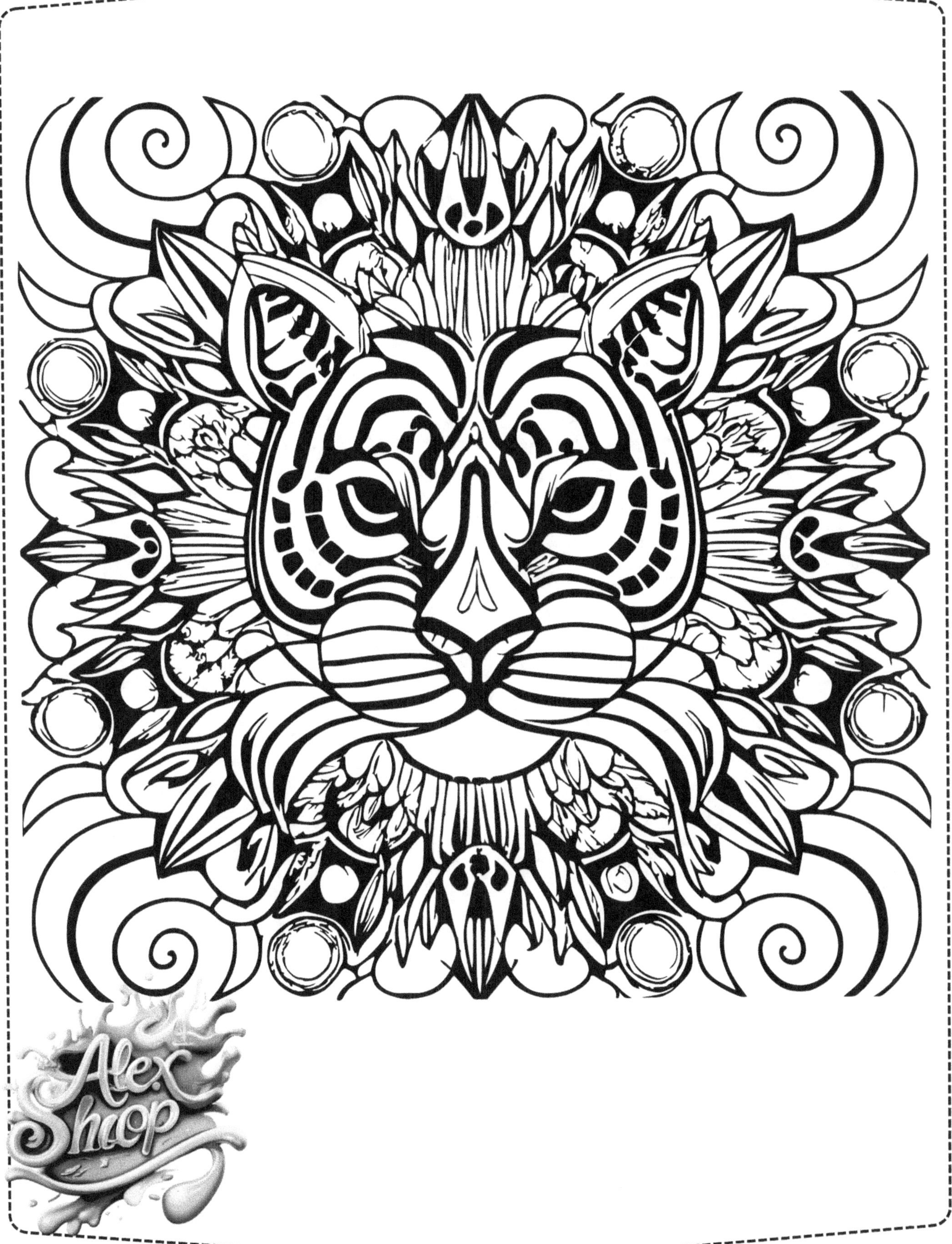
Alex
Shop

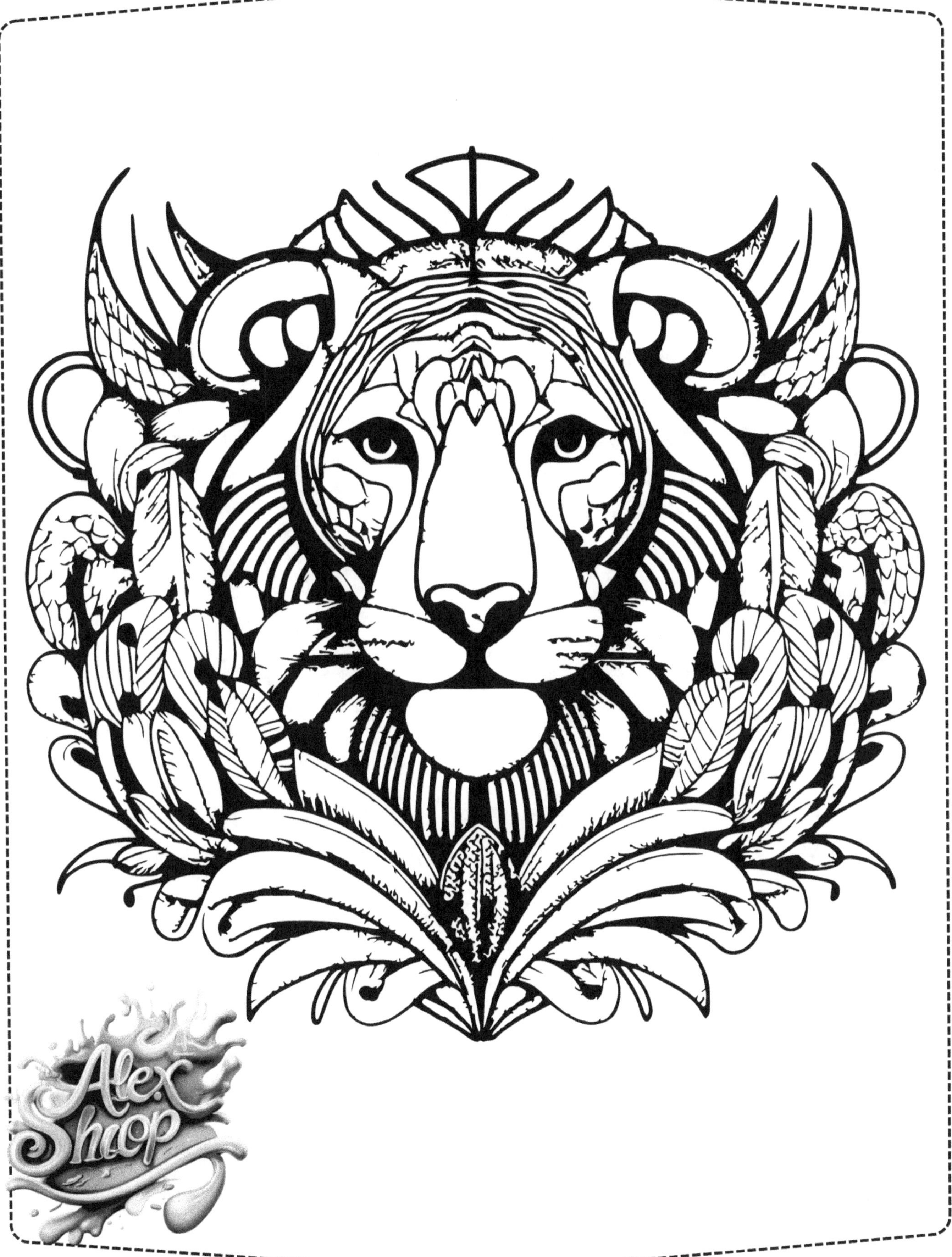
Alex
Shop

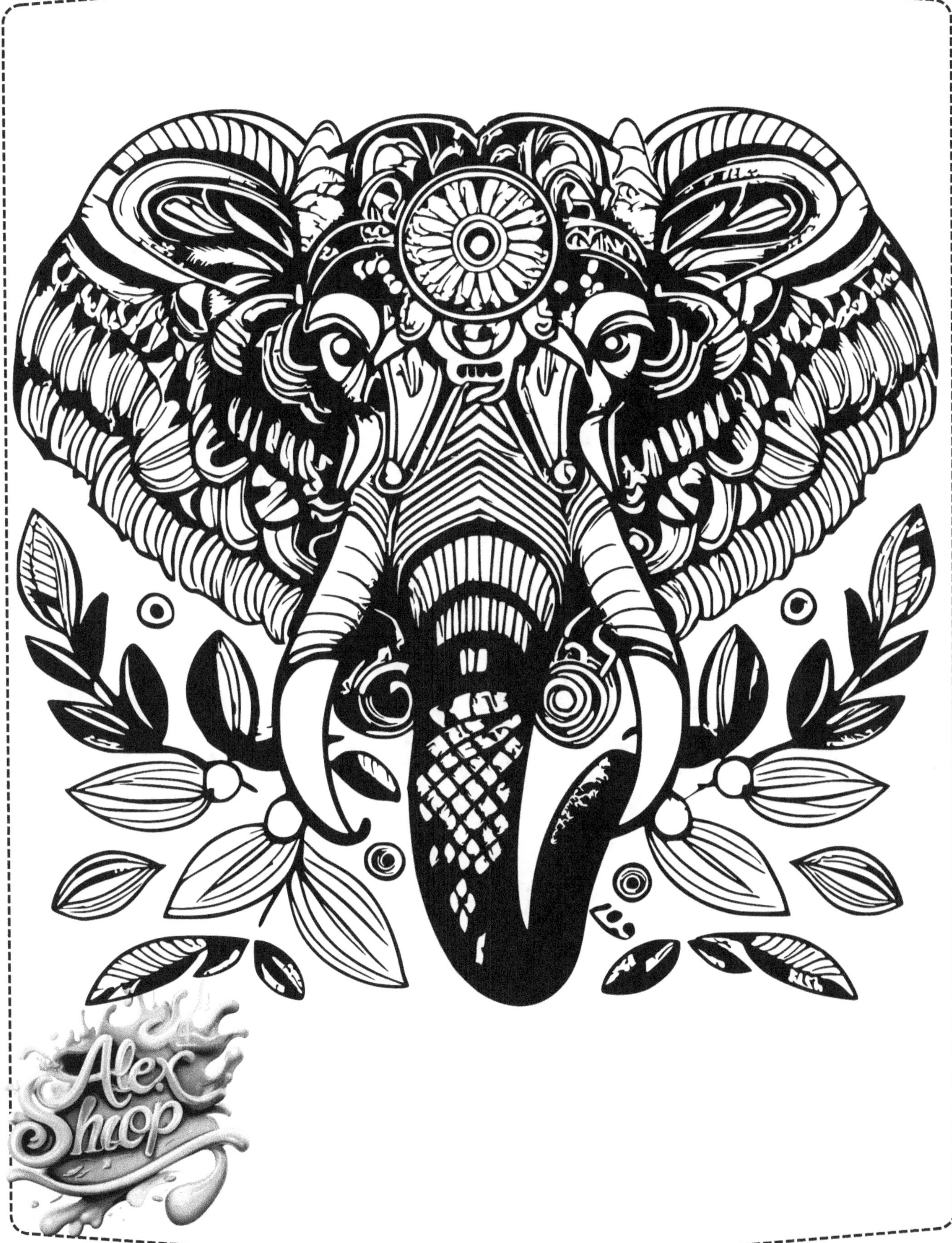
Alex
Shop

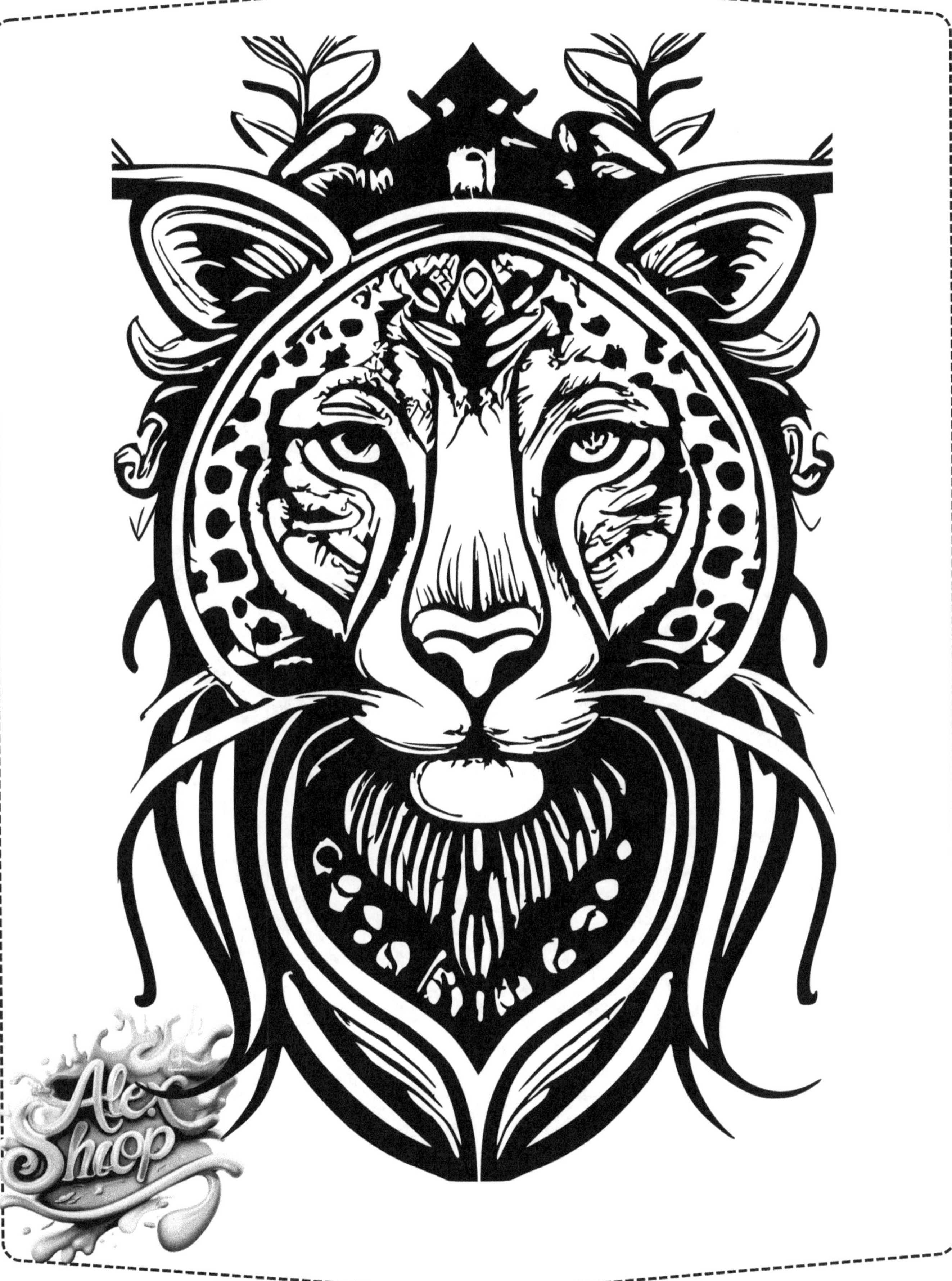
Ale
Shop

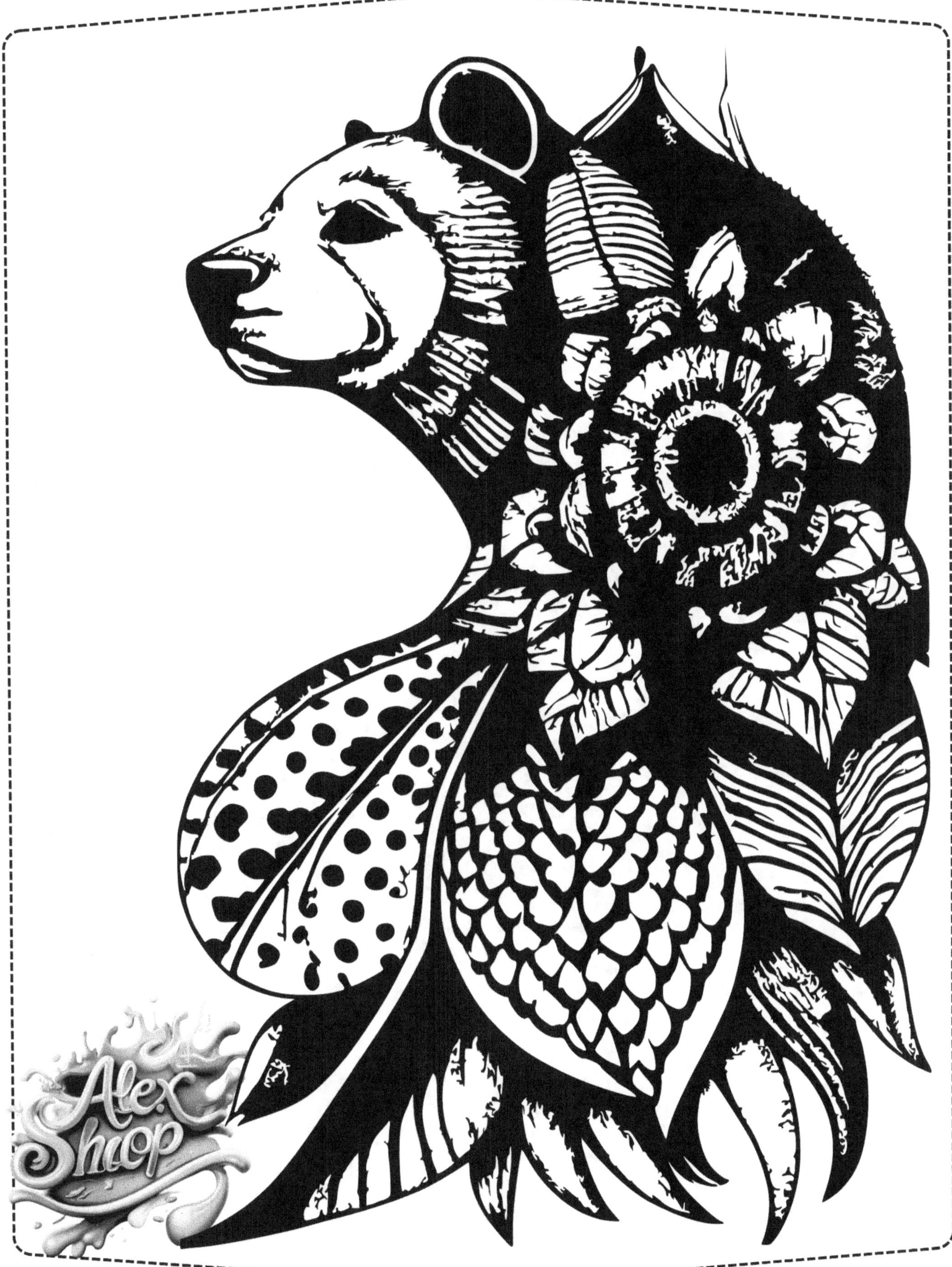
Alex
Shop

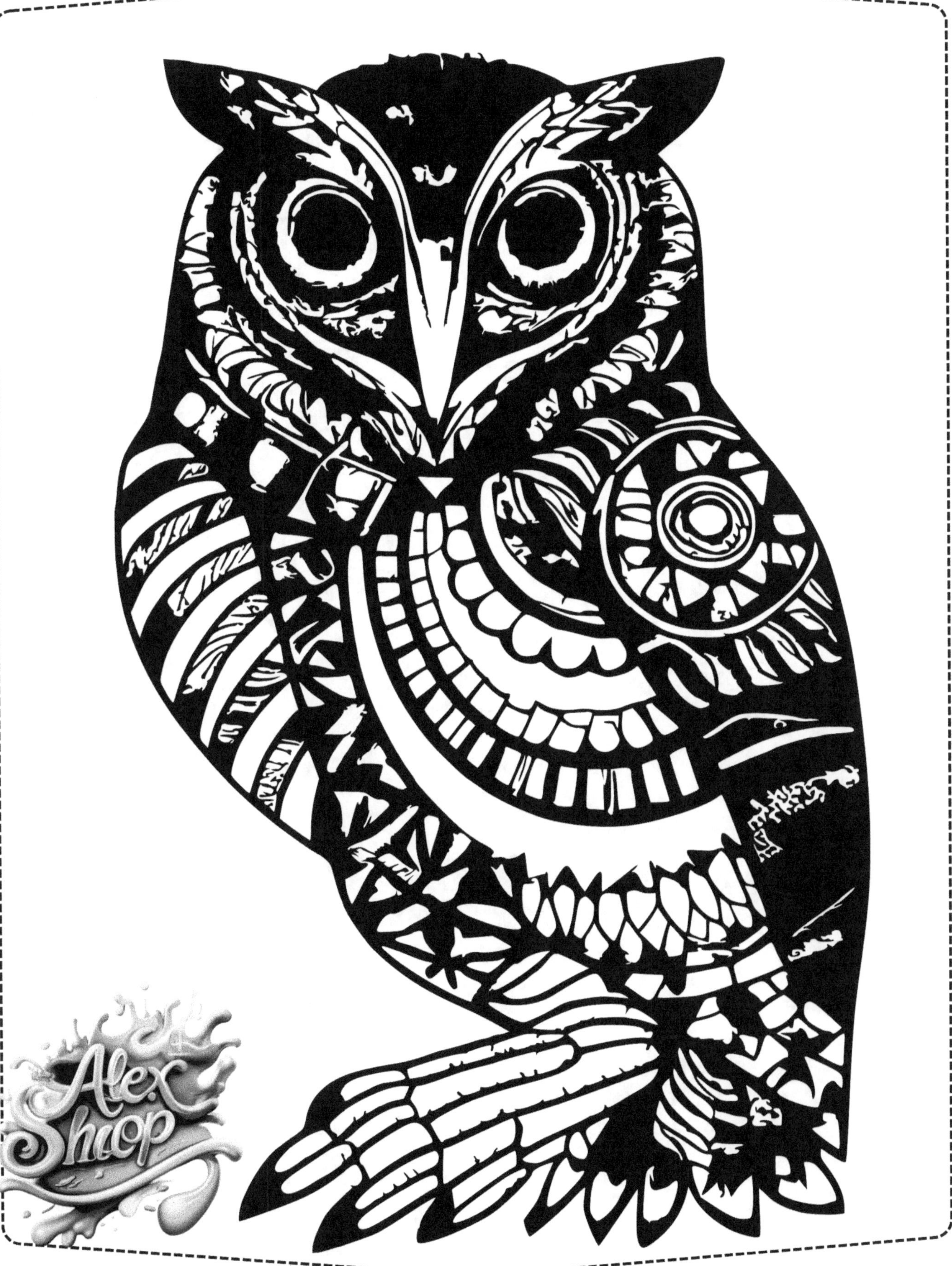
Alex
Shoop

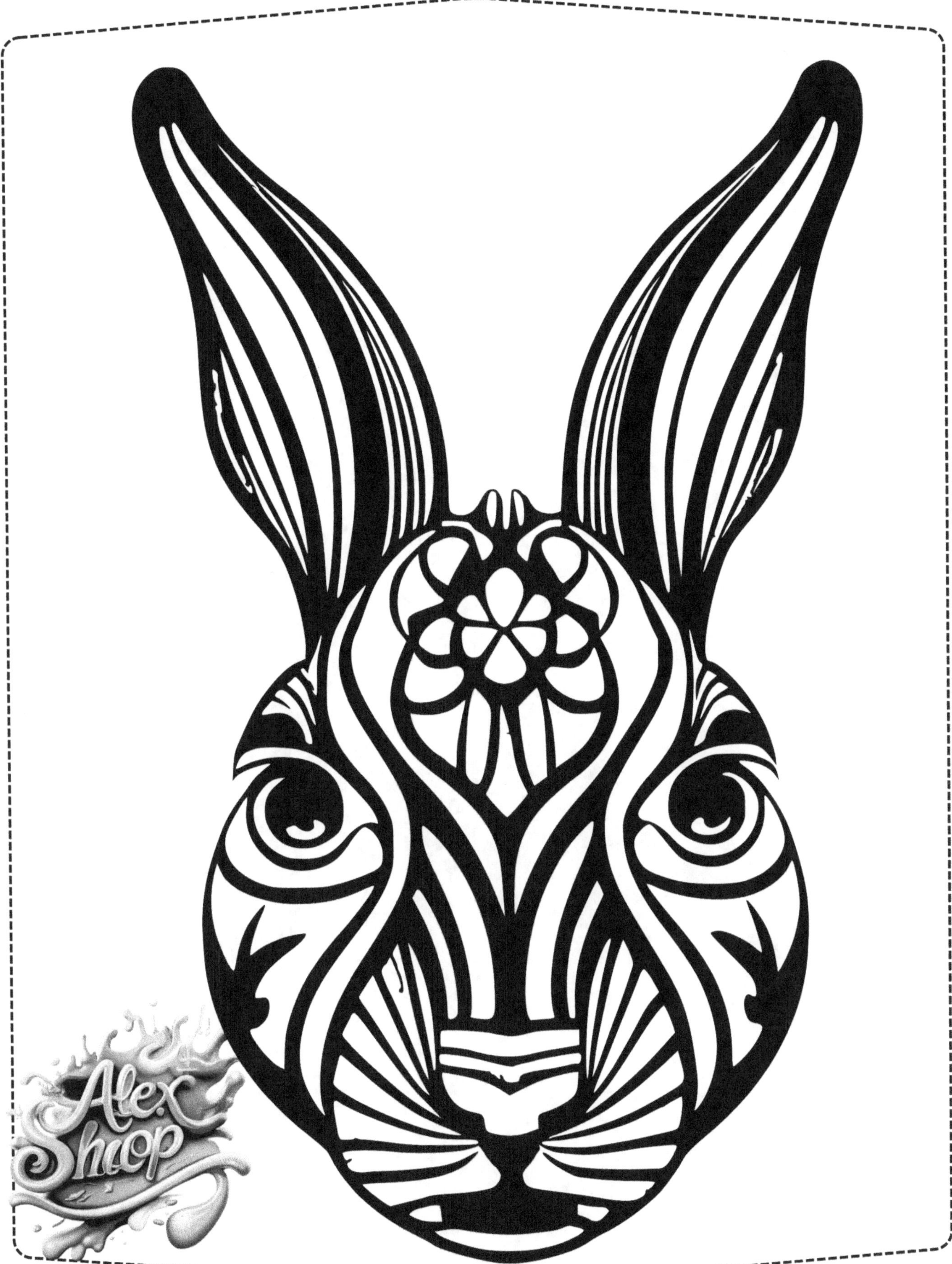
Alex
Shop

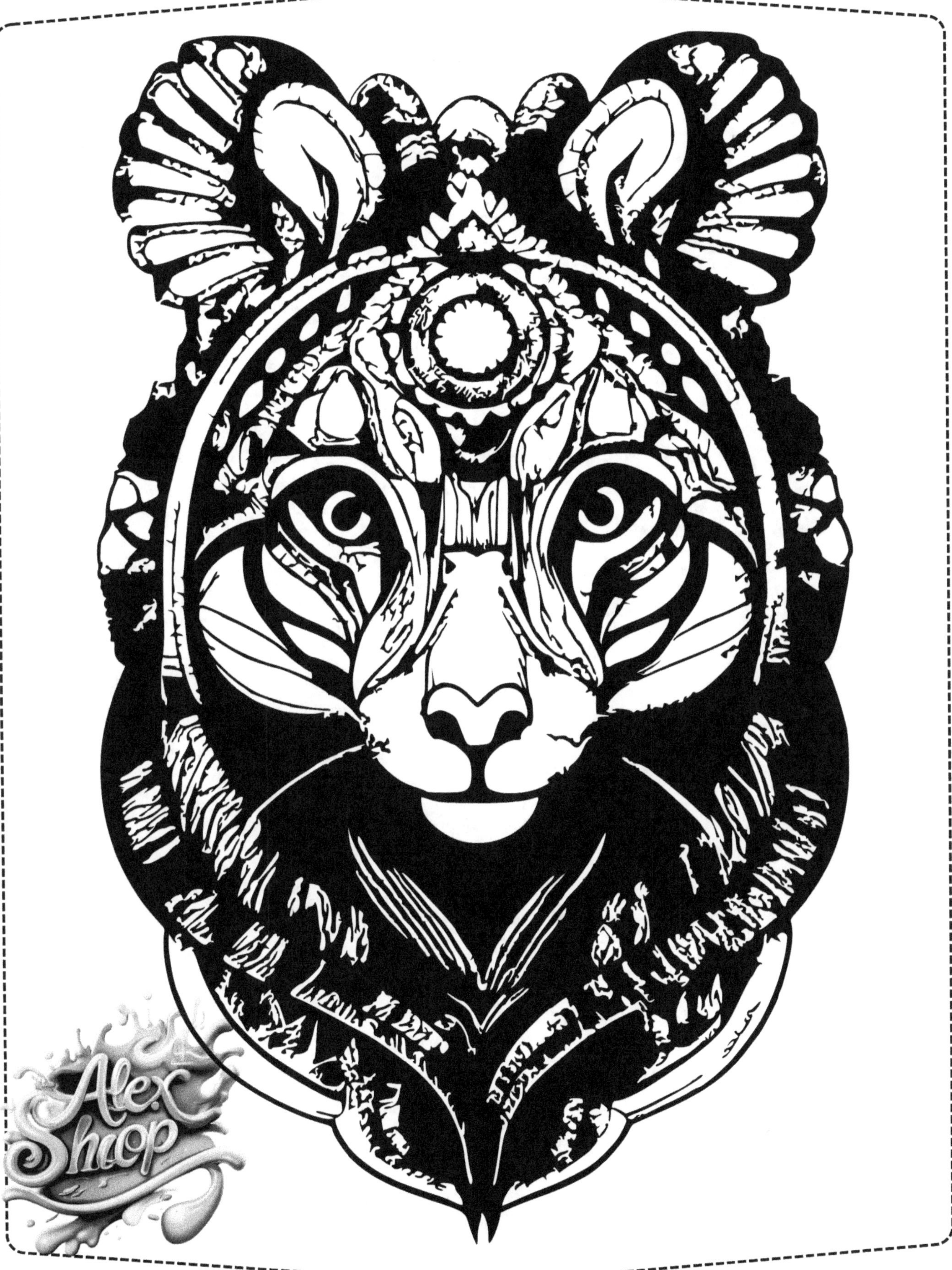
Alex
Shop

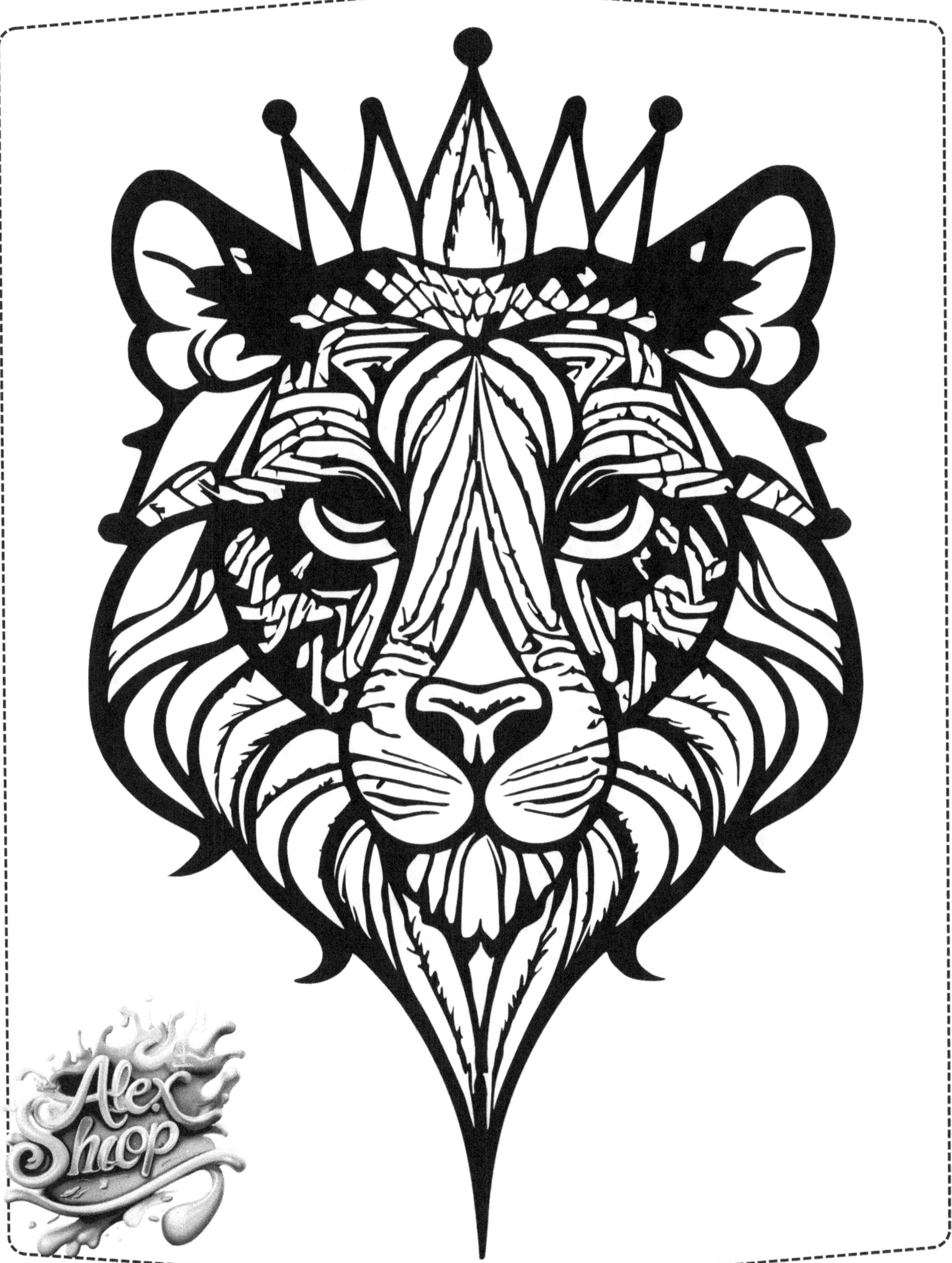

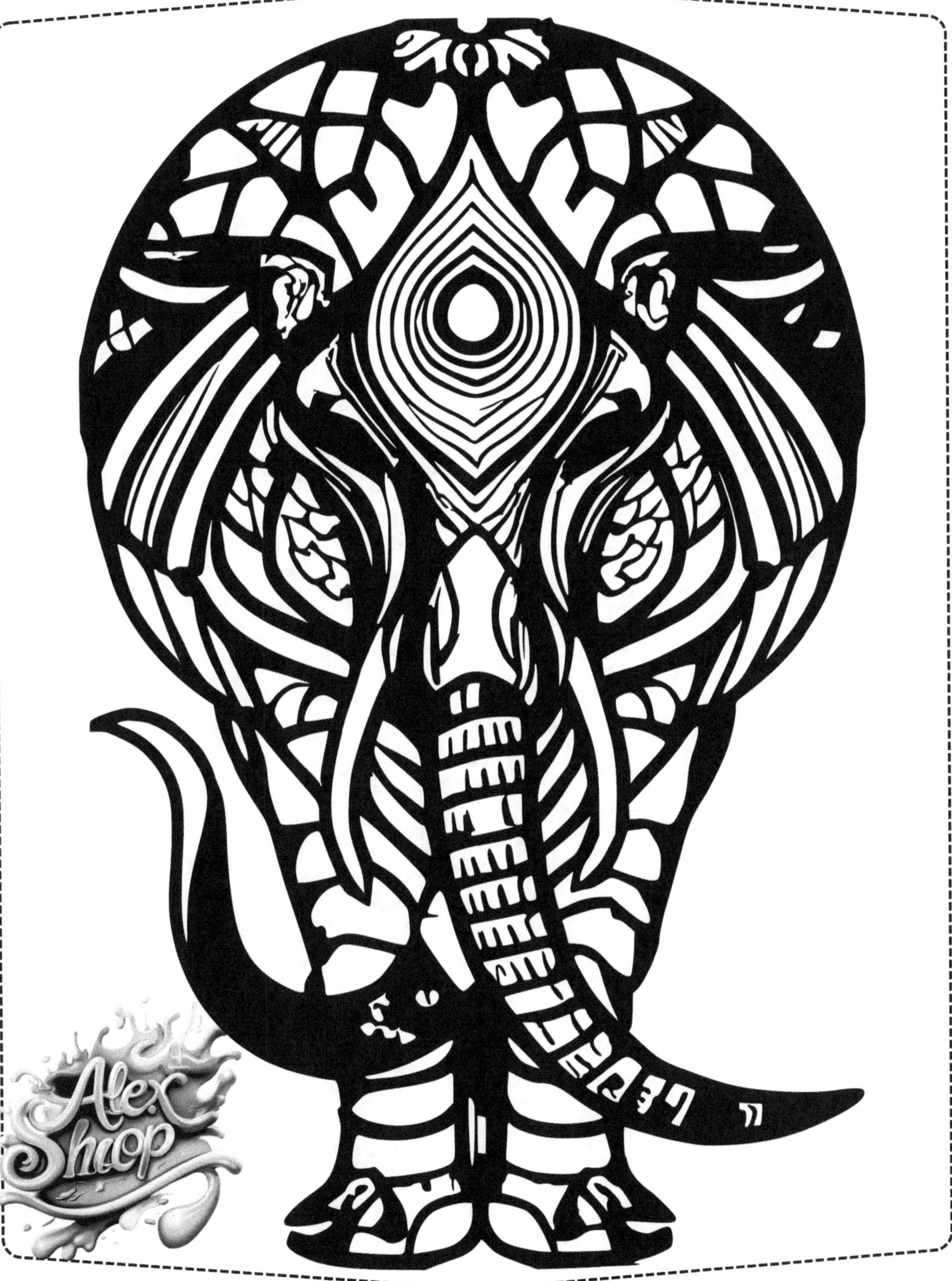
Alex
Shop

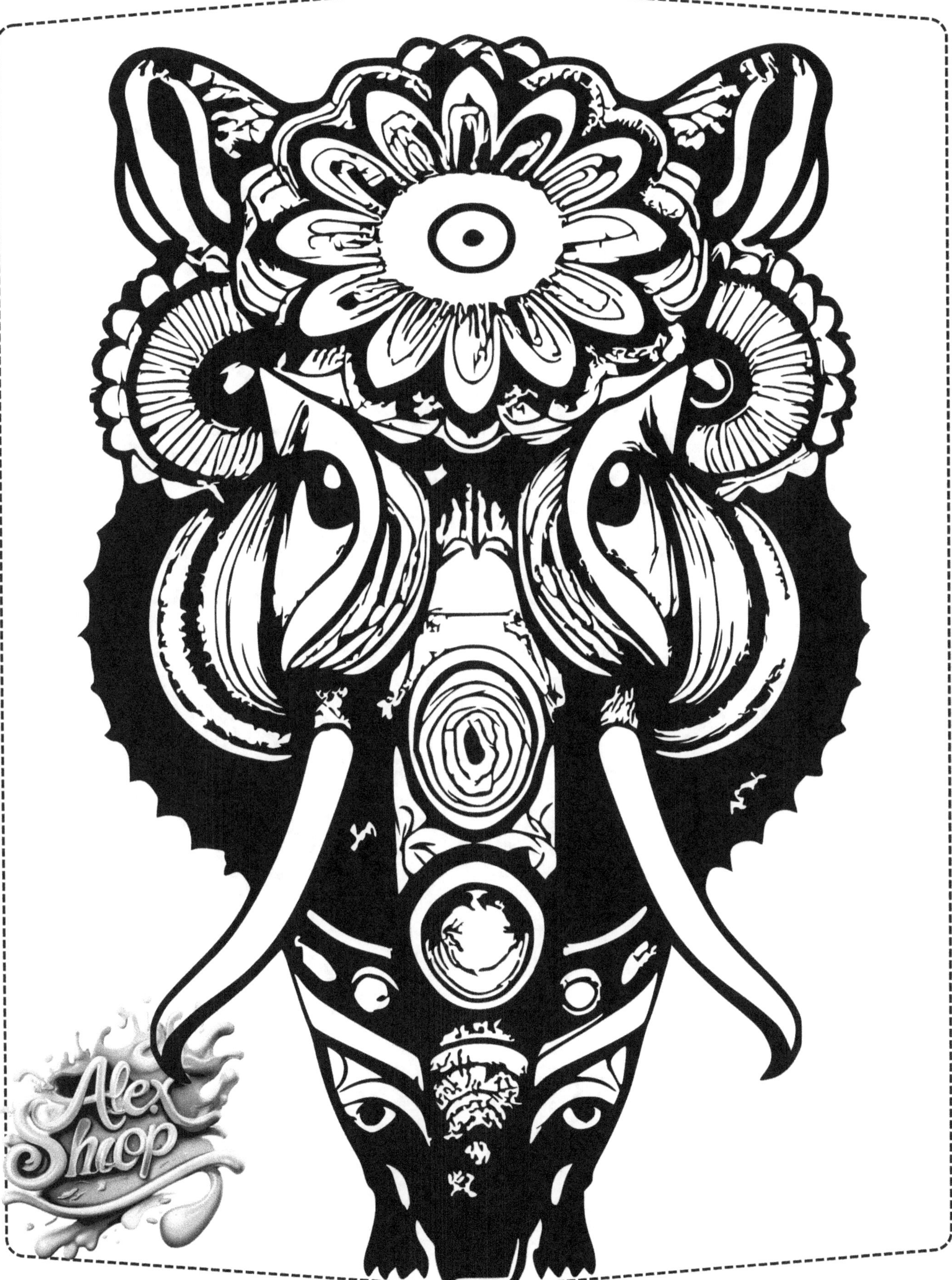
Alex
Shop

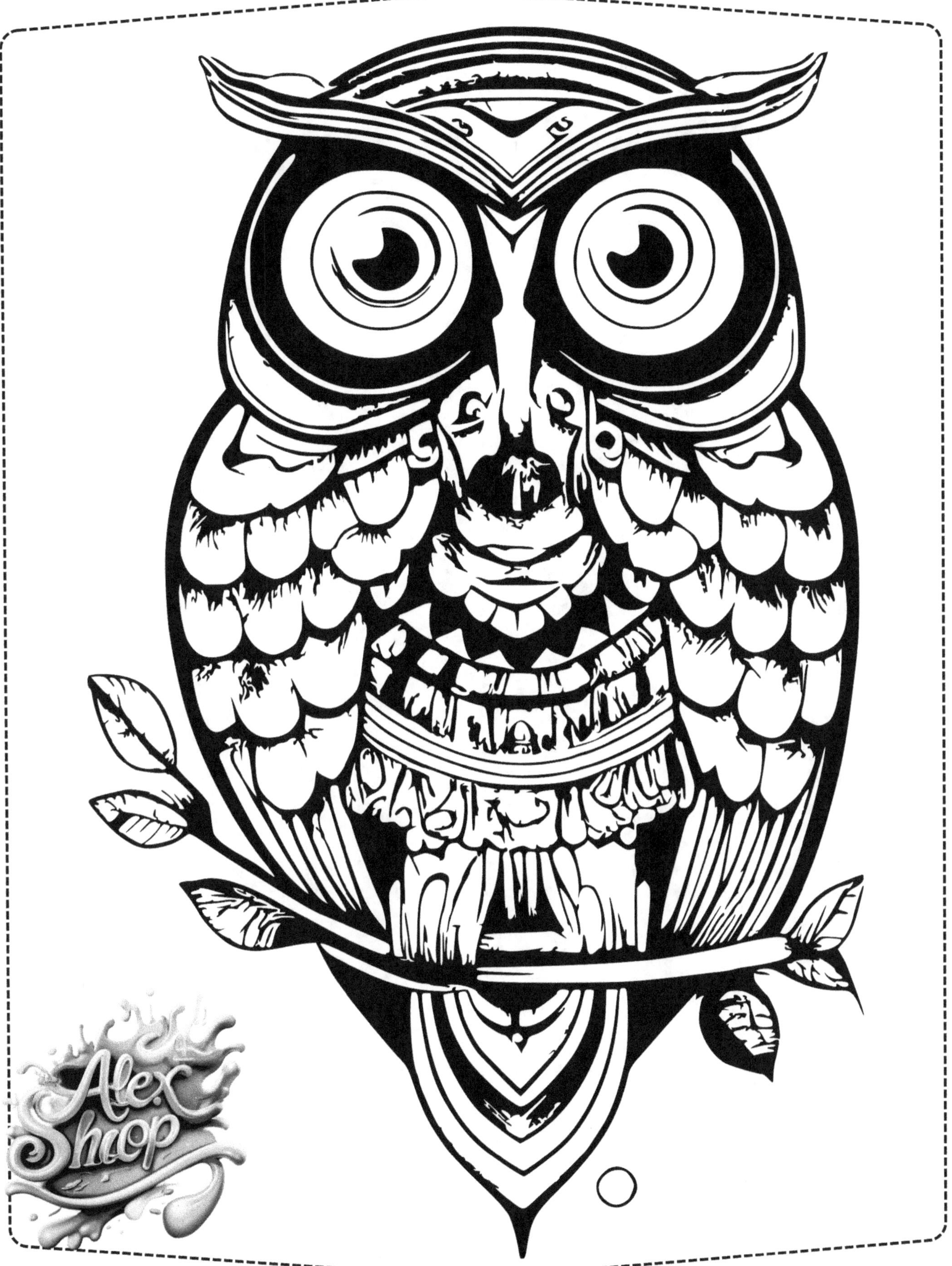

Alex
Shop

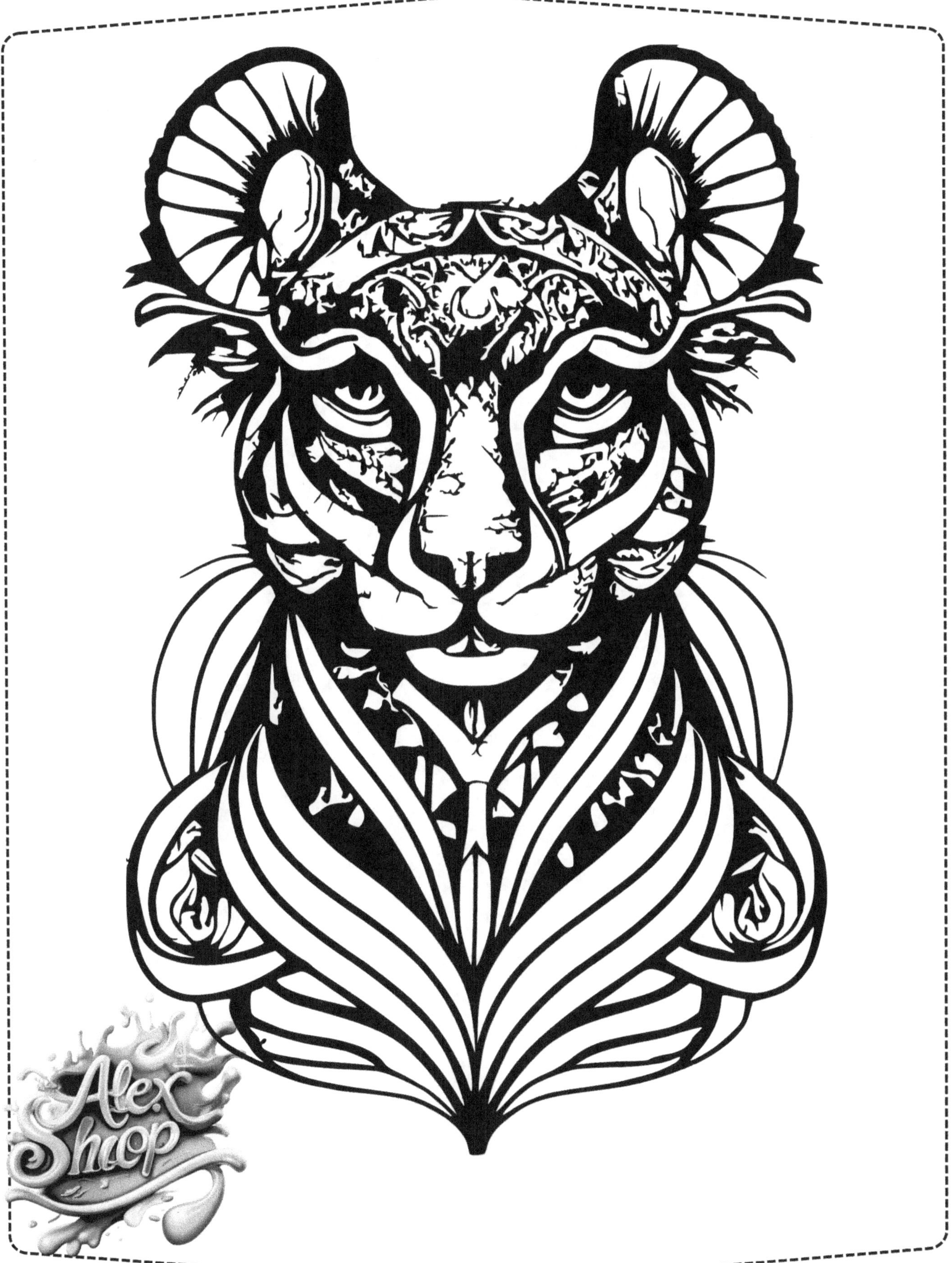
Alex
Shop

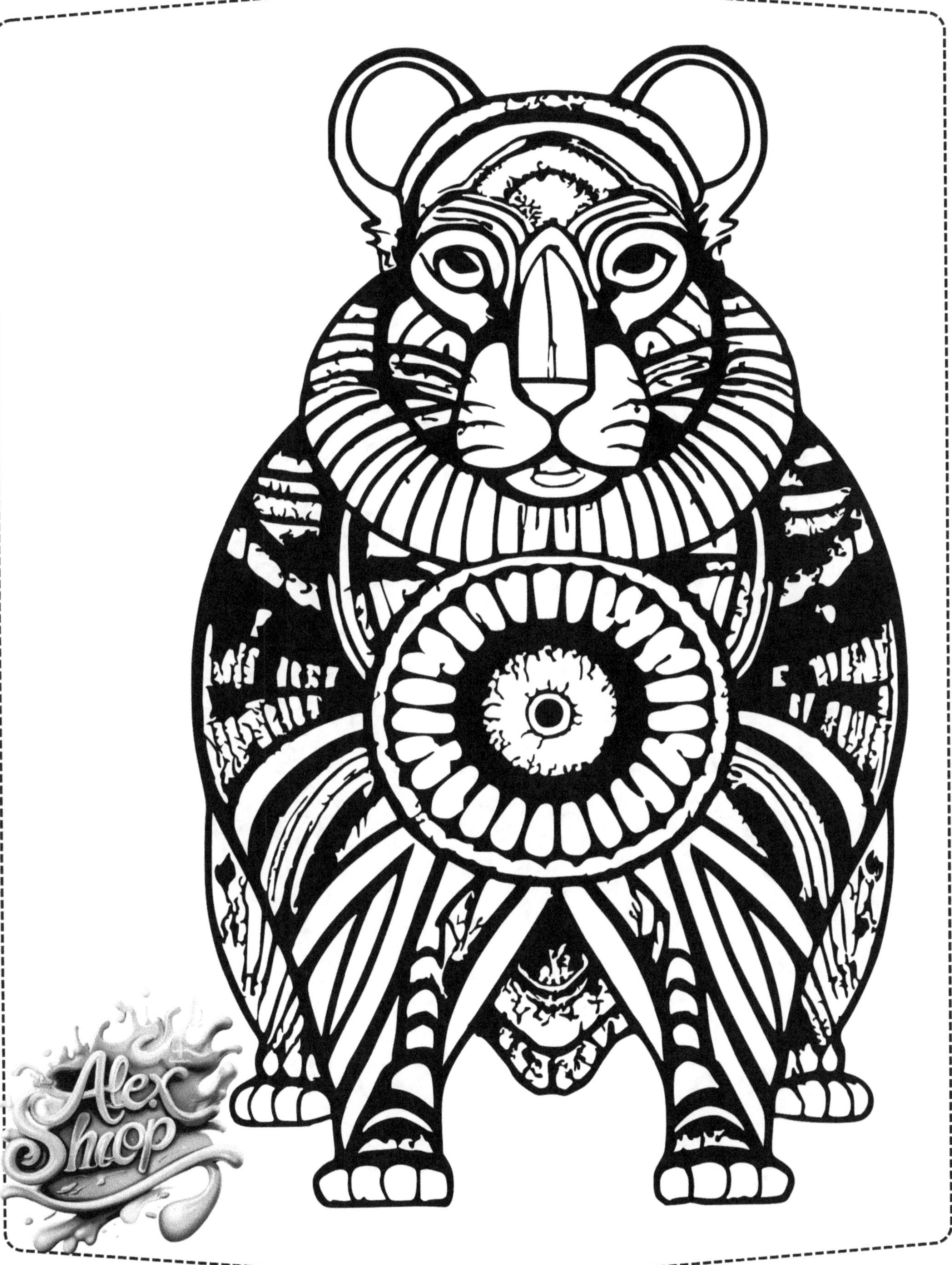
Alex
Shop

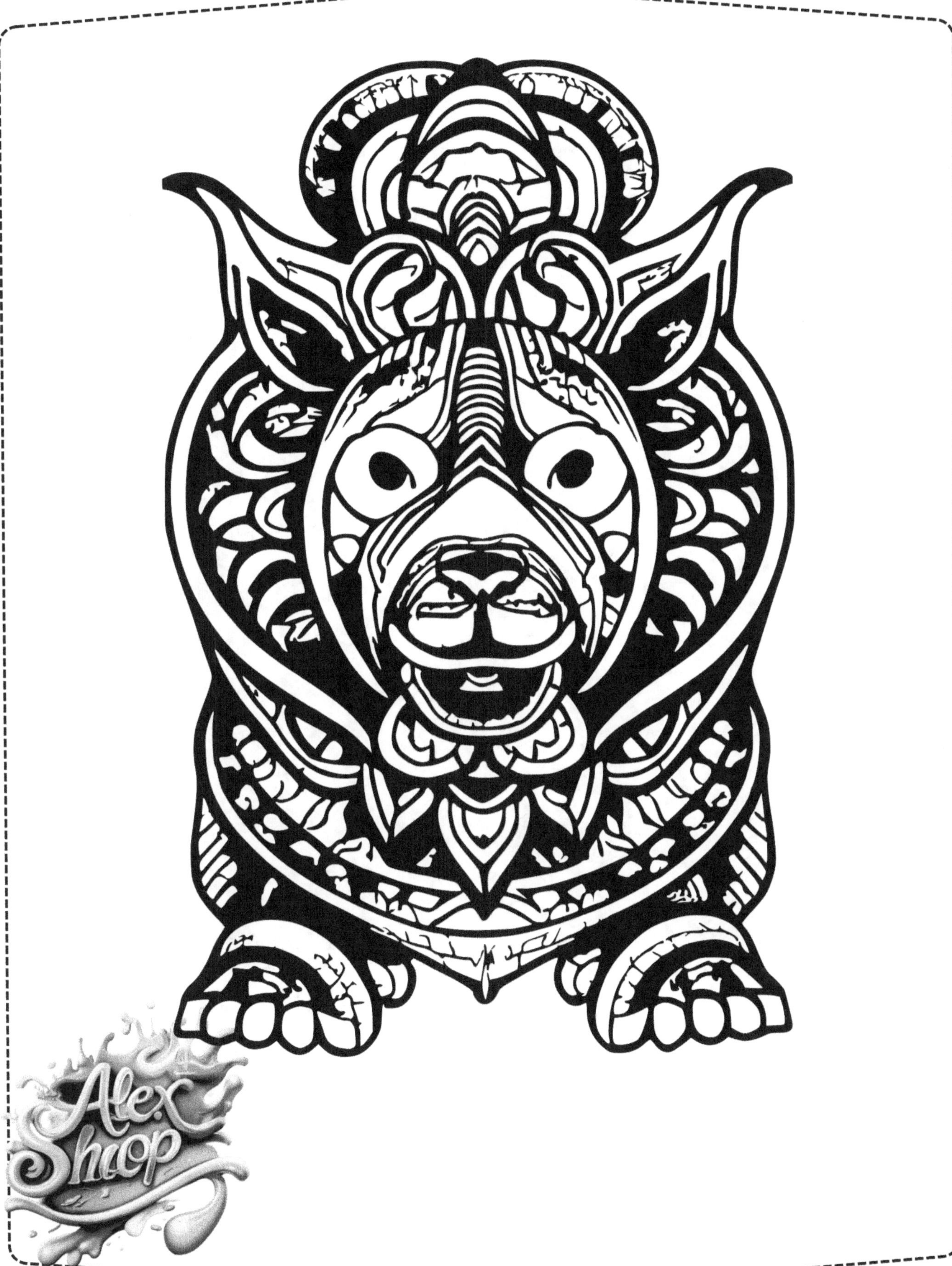
Alex
Shop

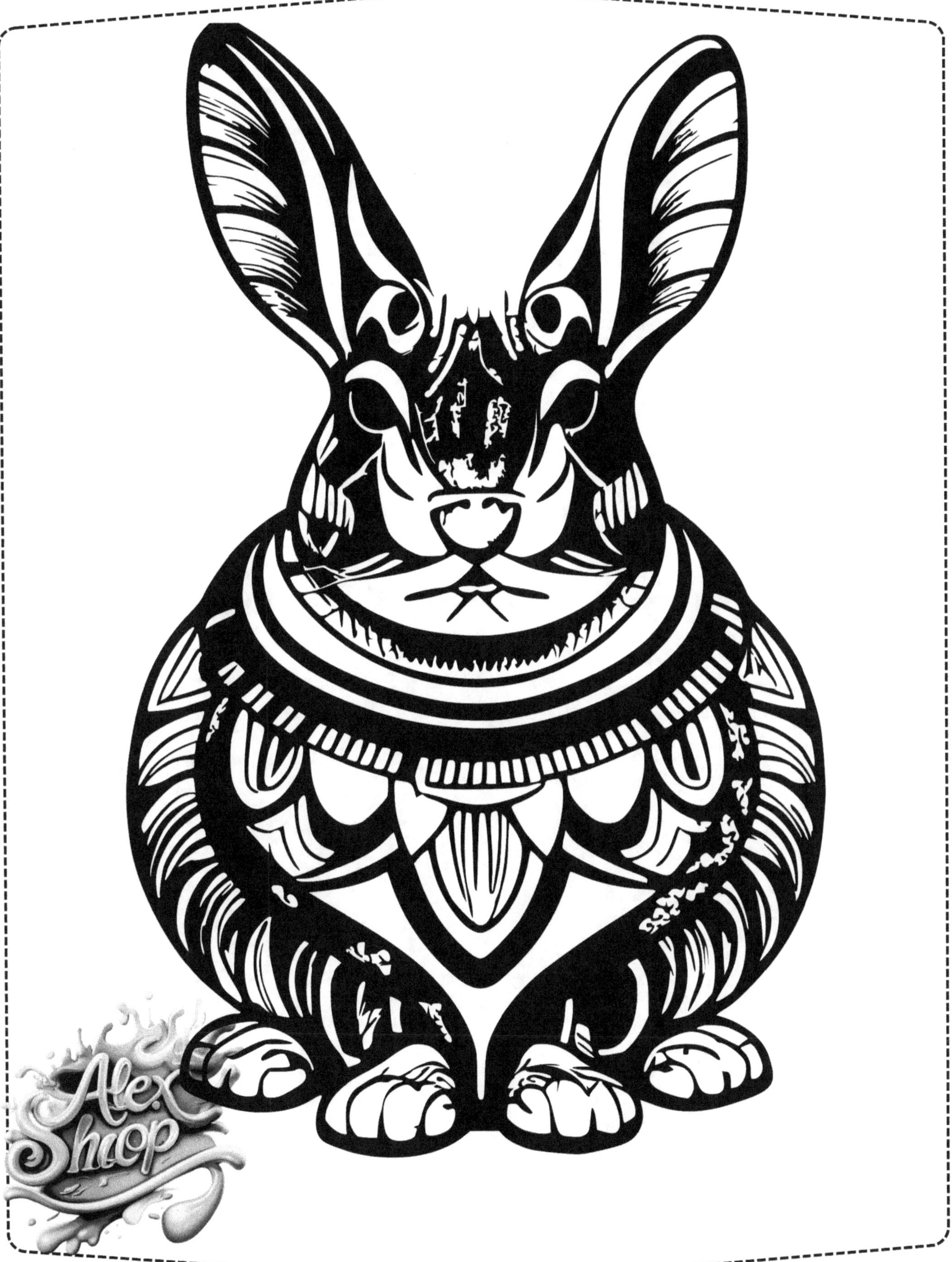
Alex
Shop

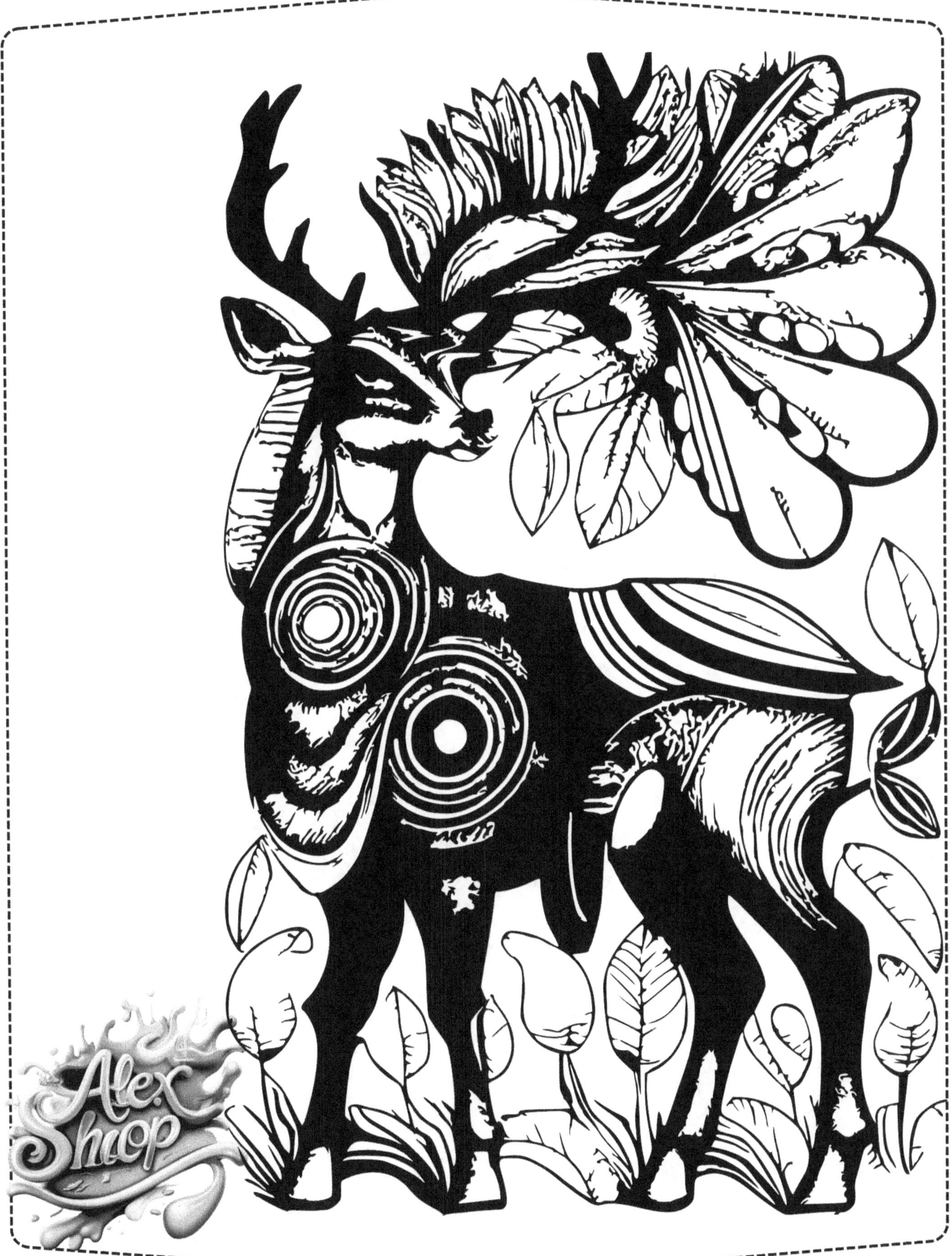
Alex
Shop

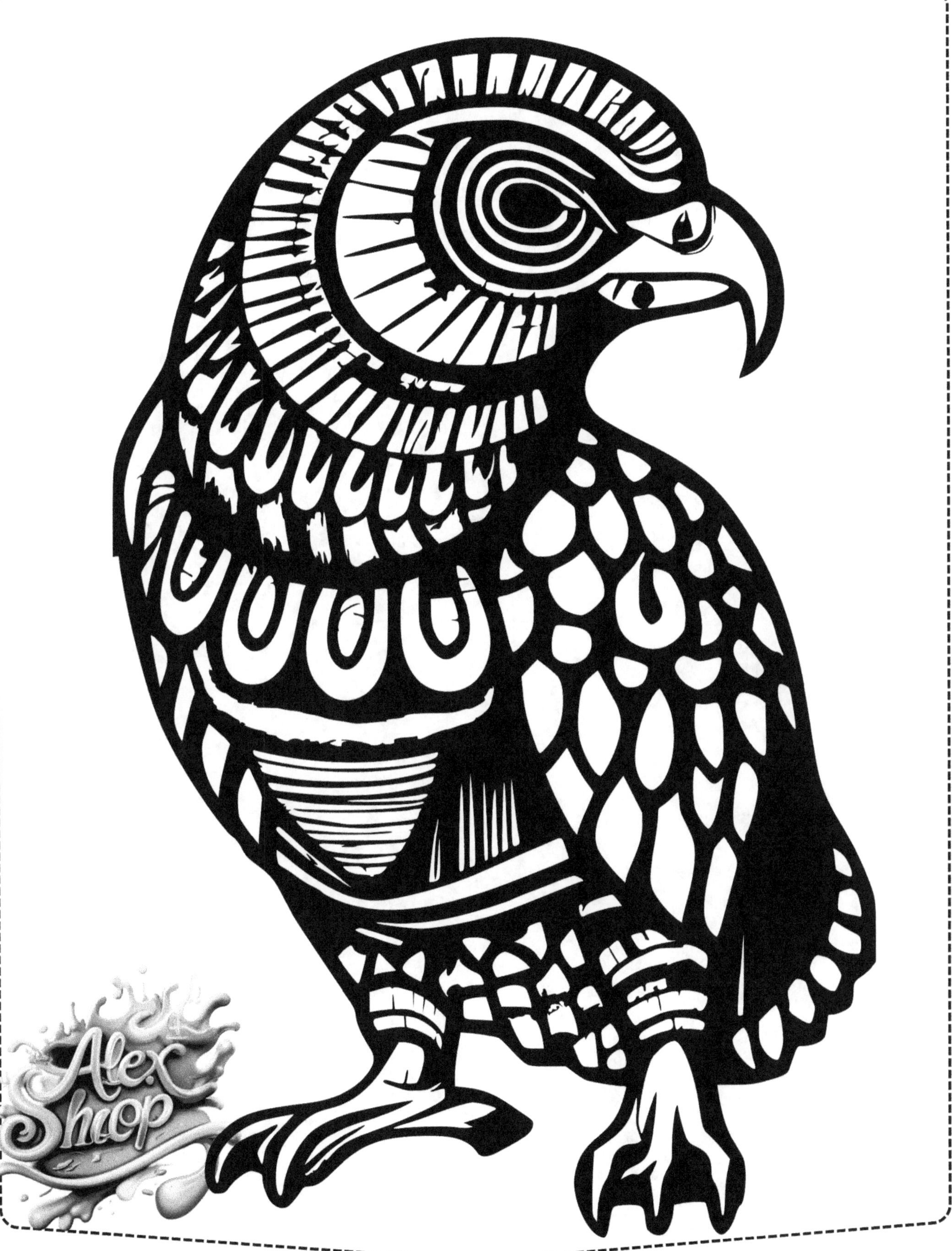
Alex
Shop

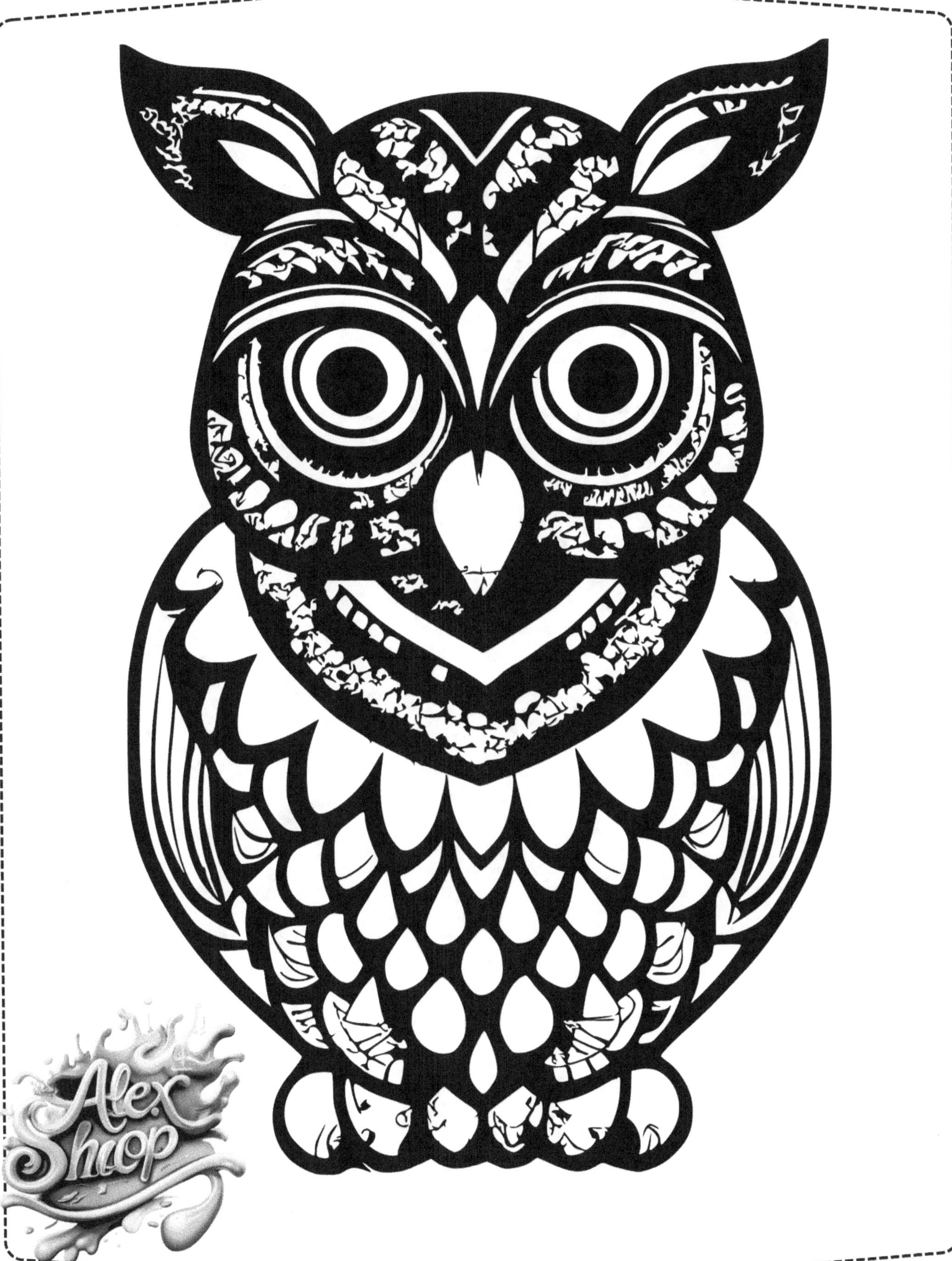
Alex
Shop

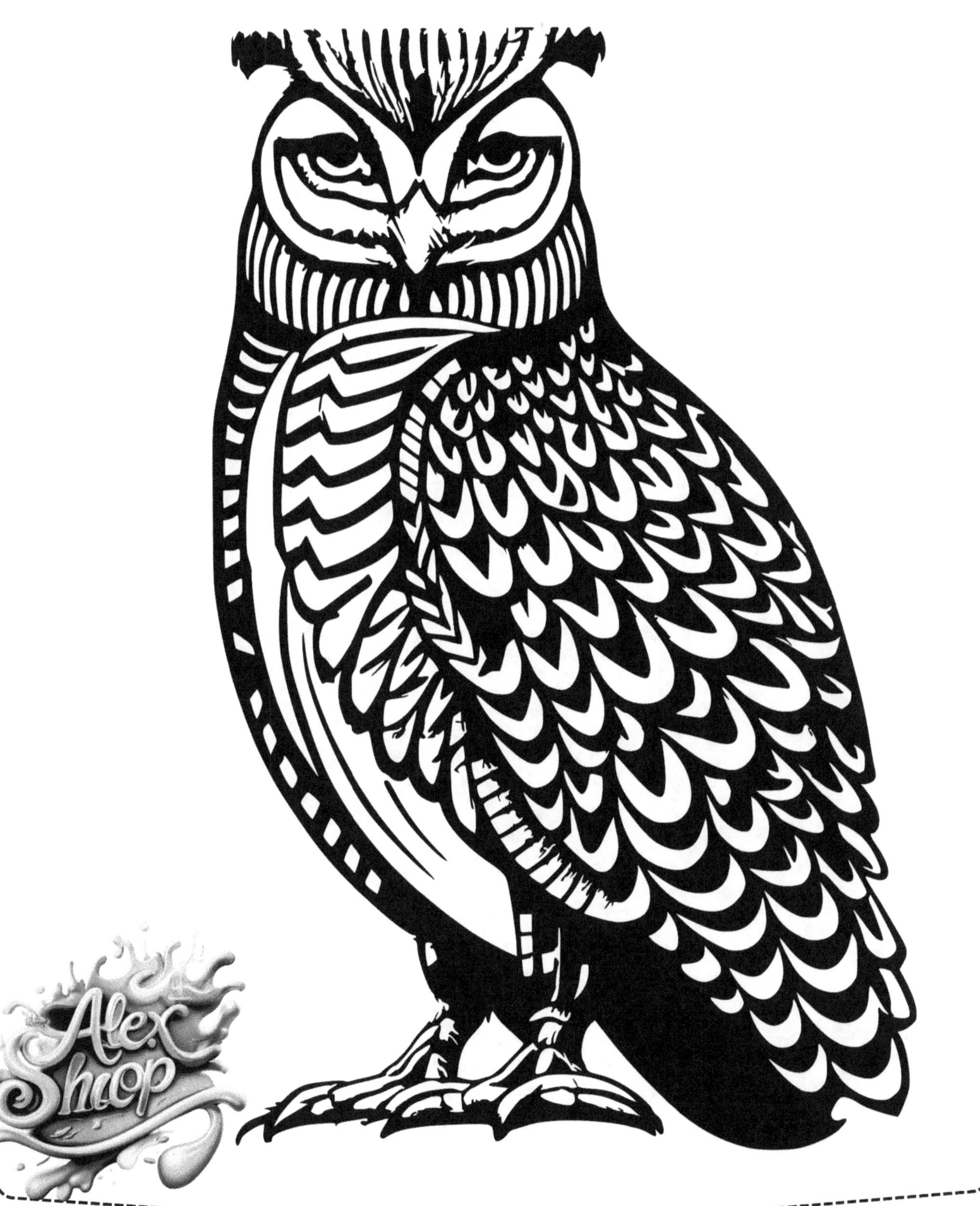

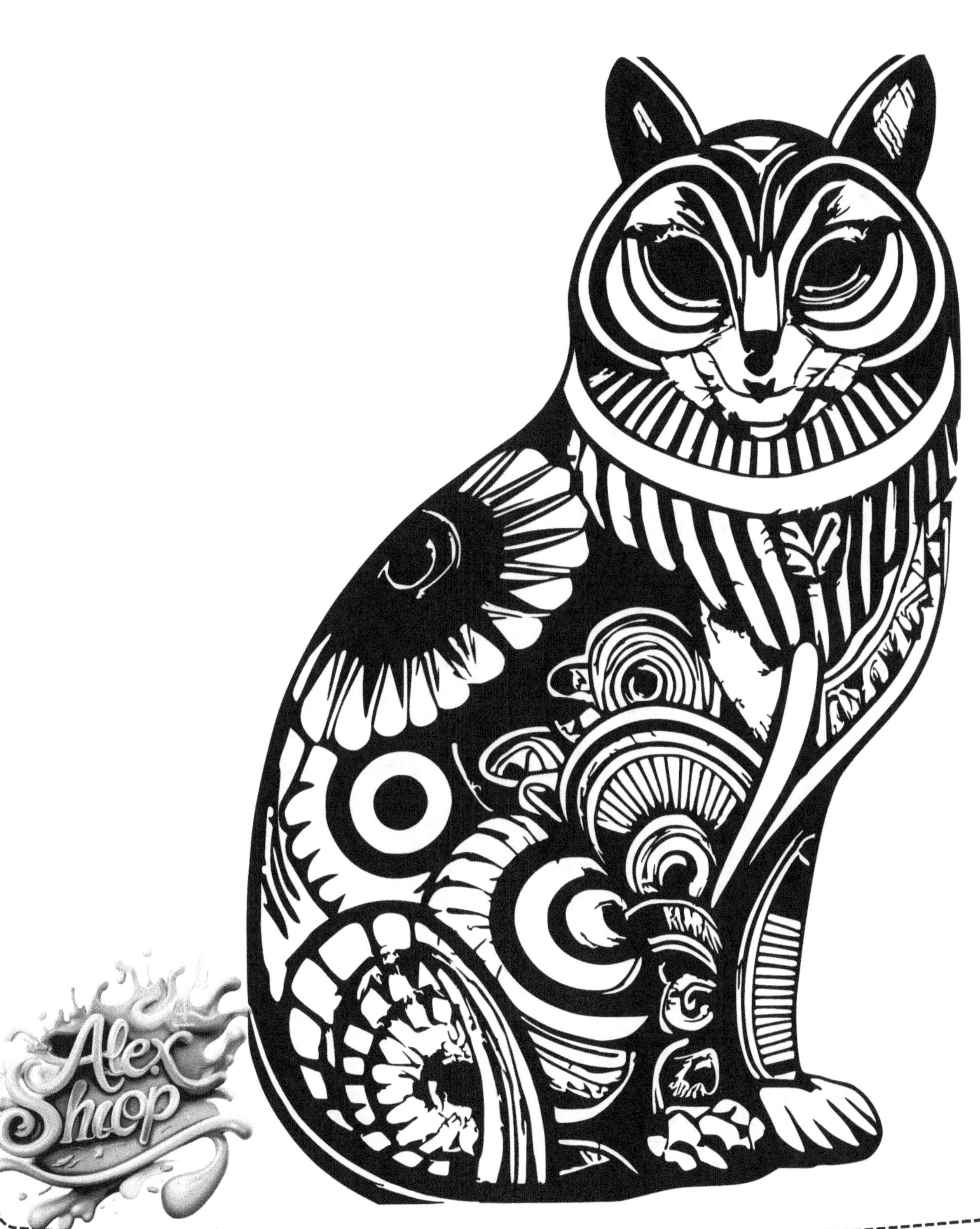

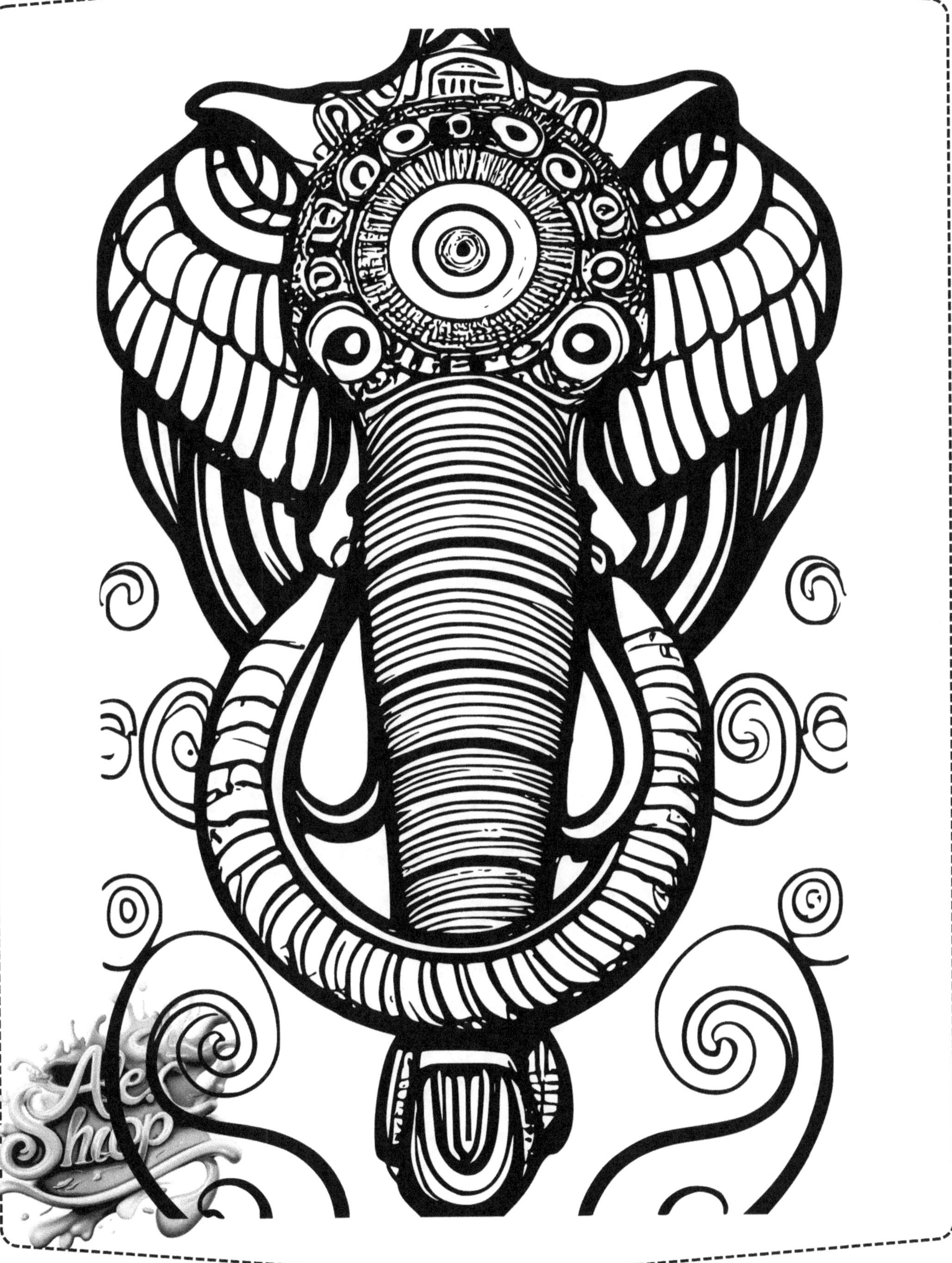

A.e.
Shop

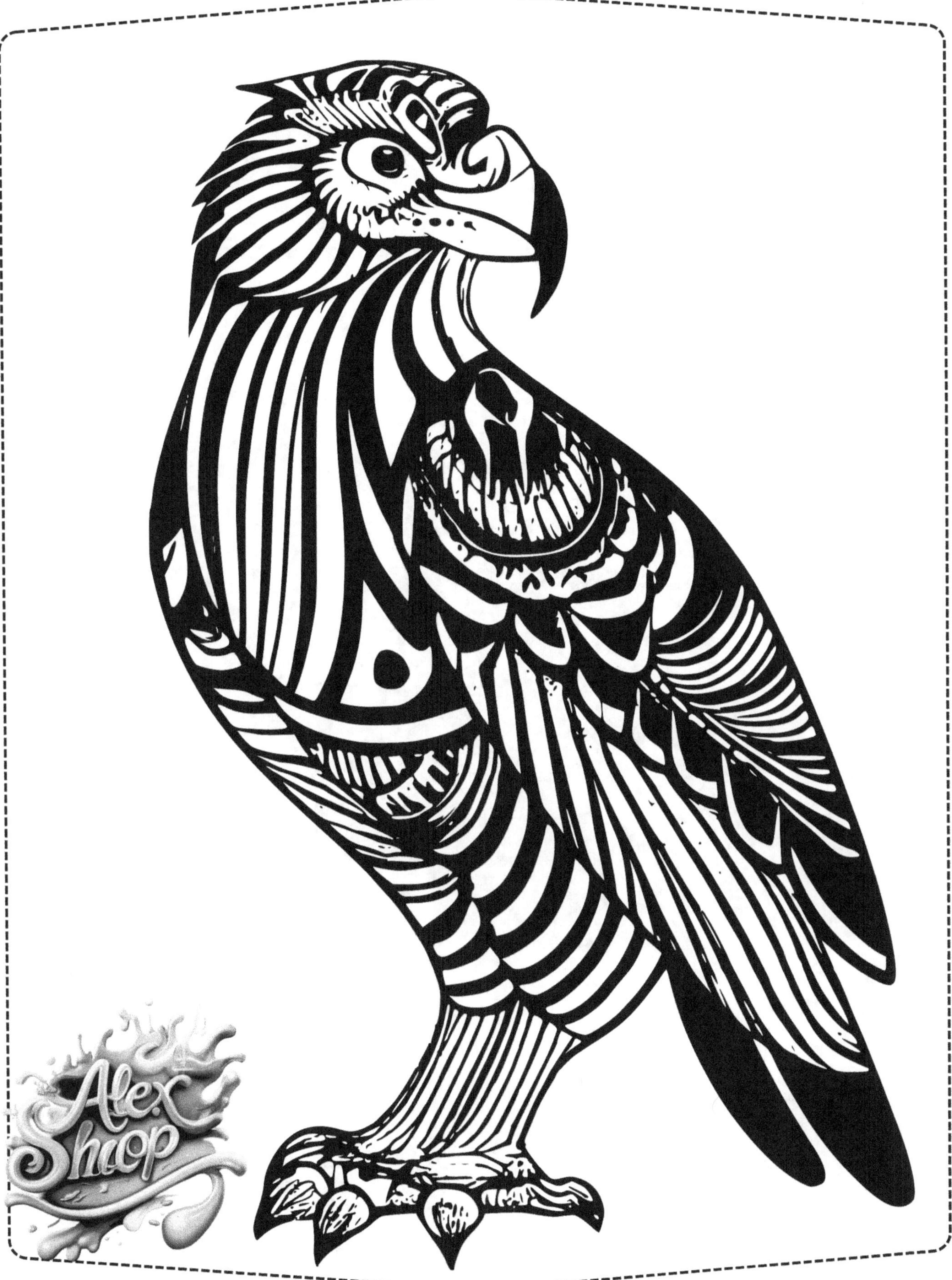
Alex
Shoop

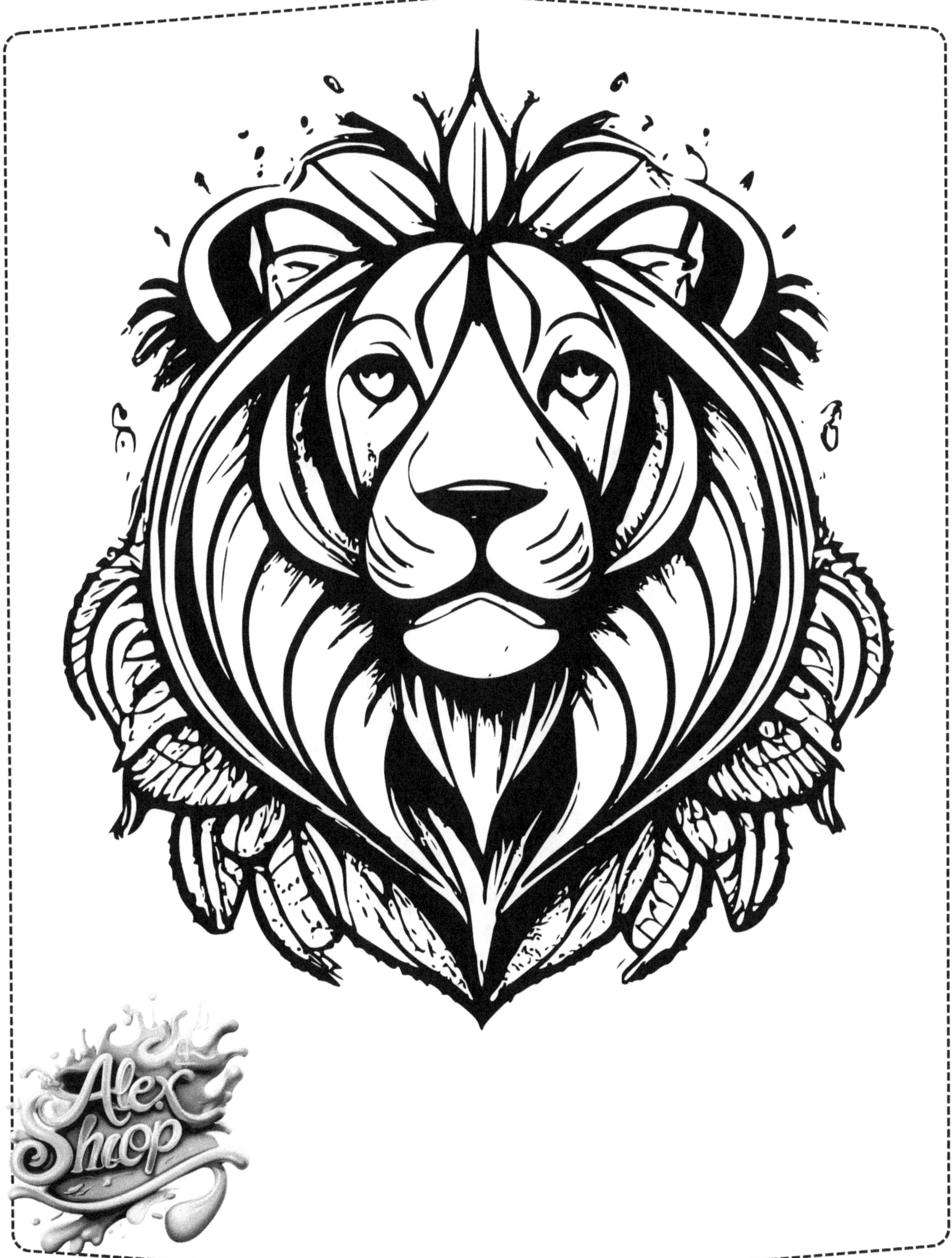
Alex
Shop

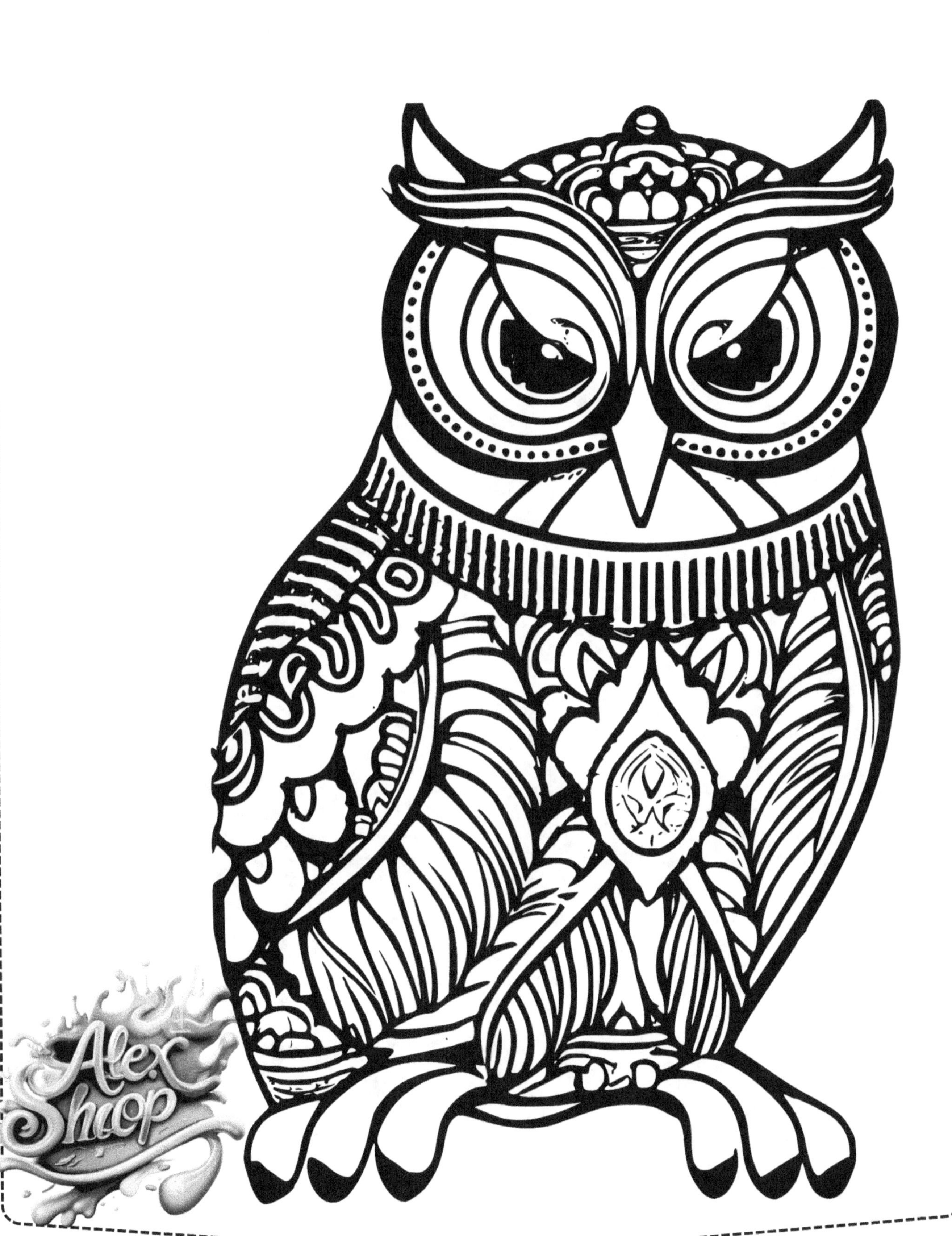
Alex
Shop

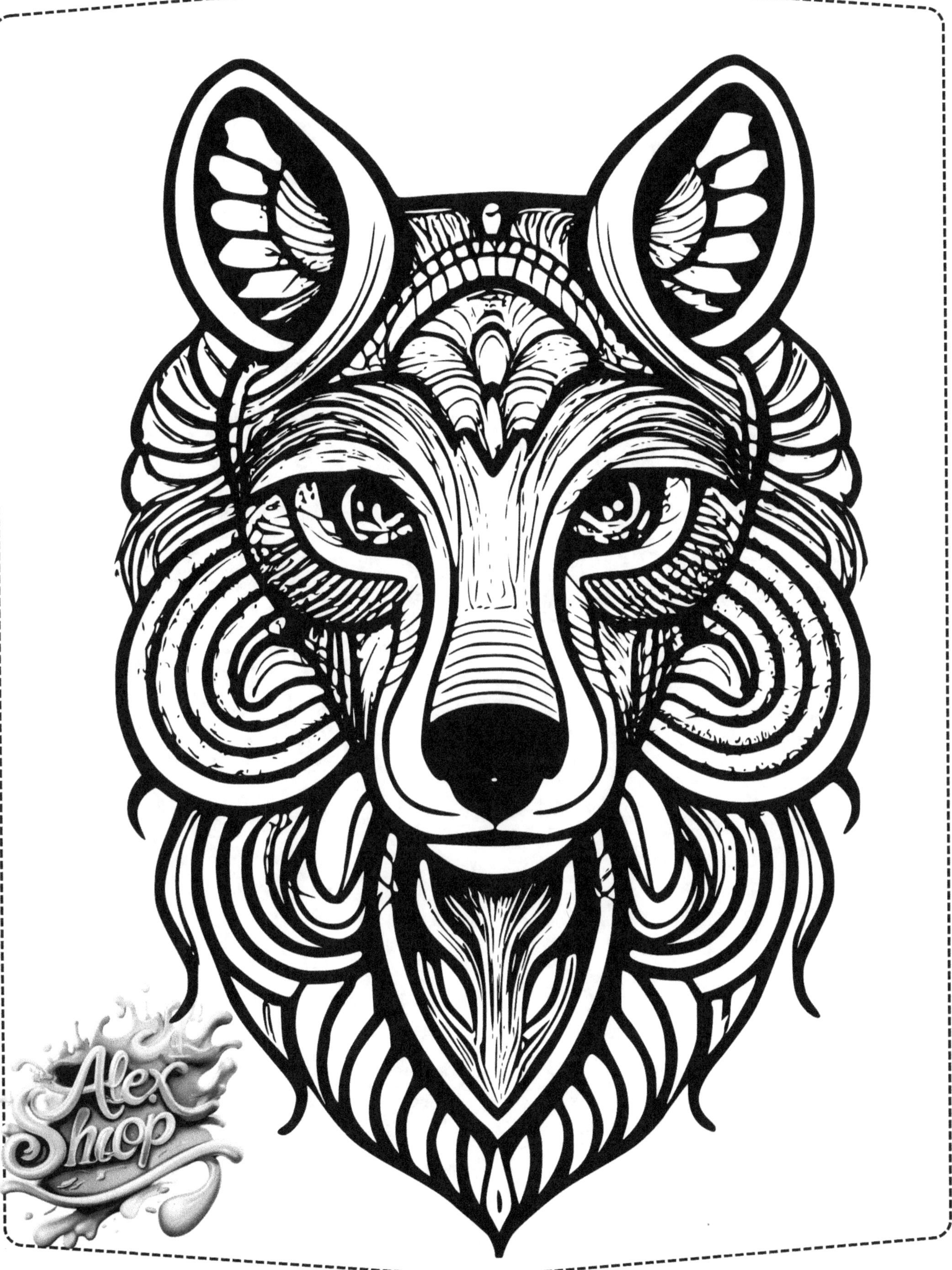
Alex
Shoop

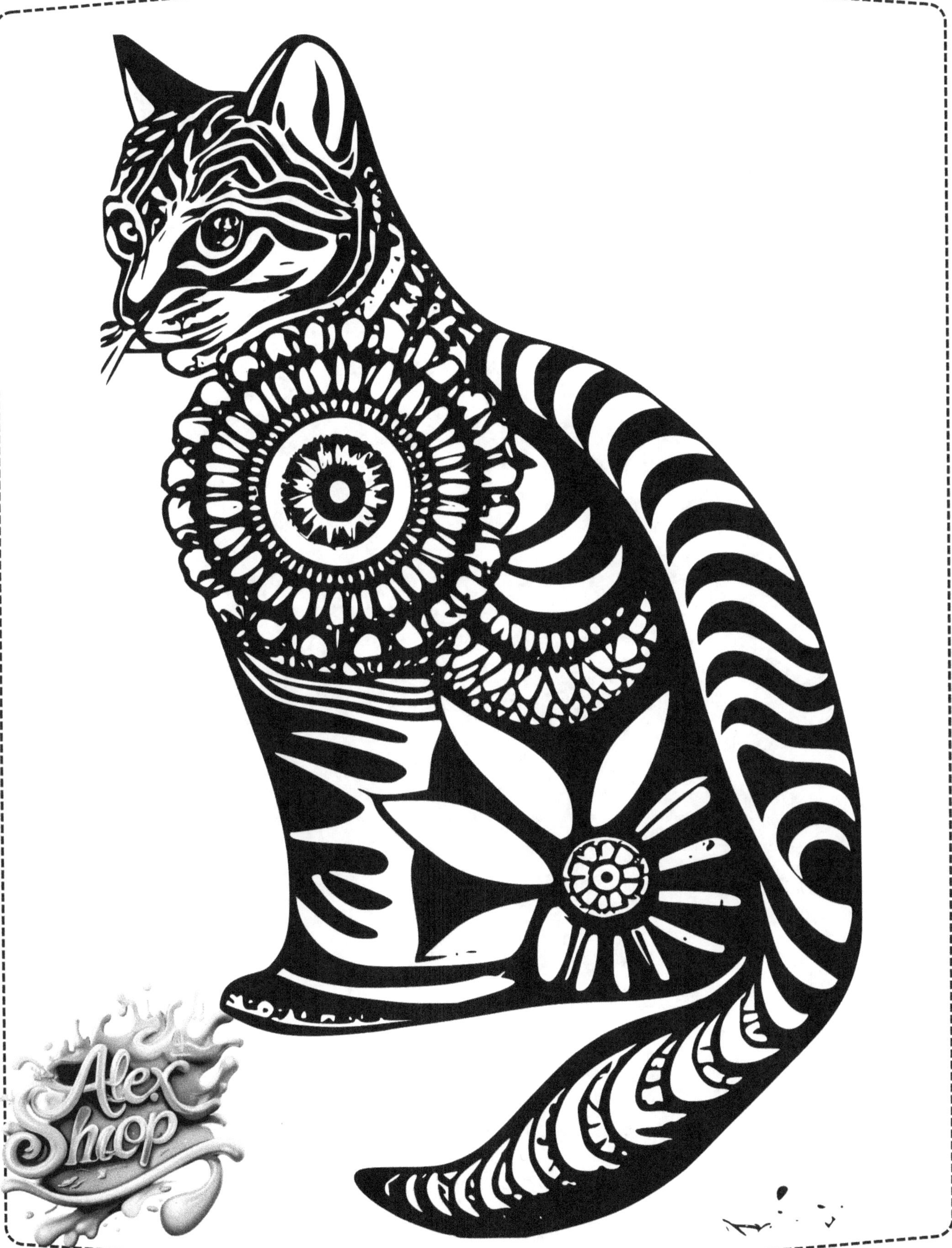
Alex
Shop

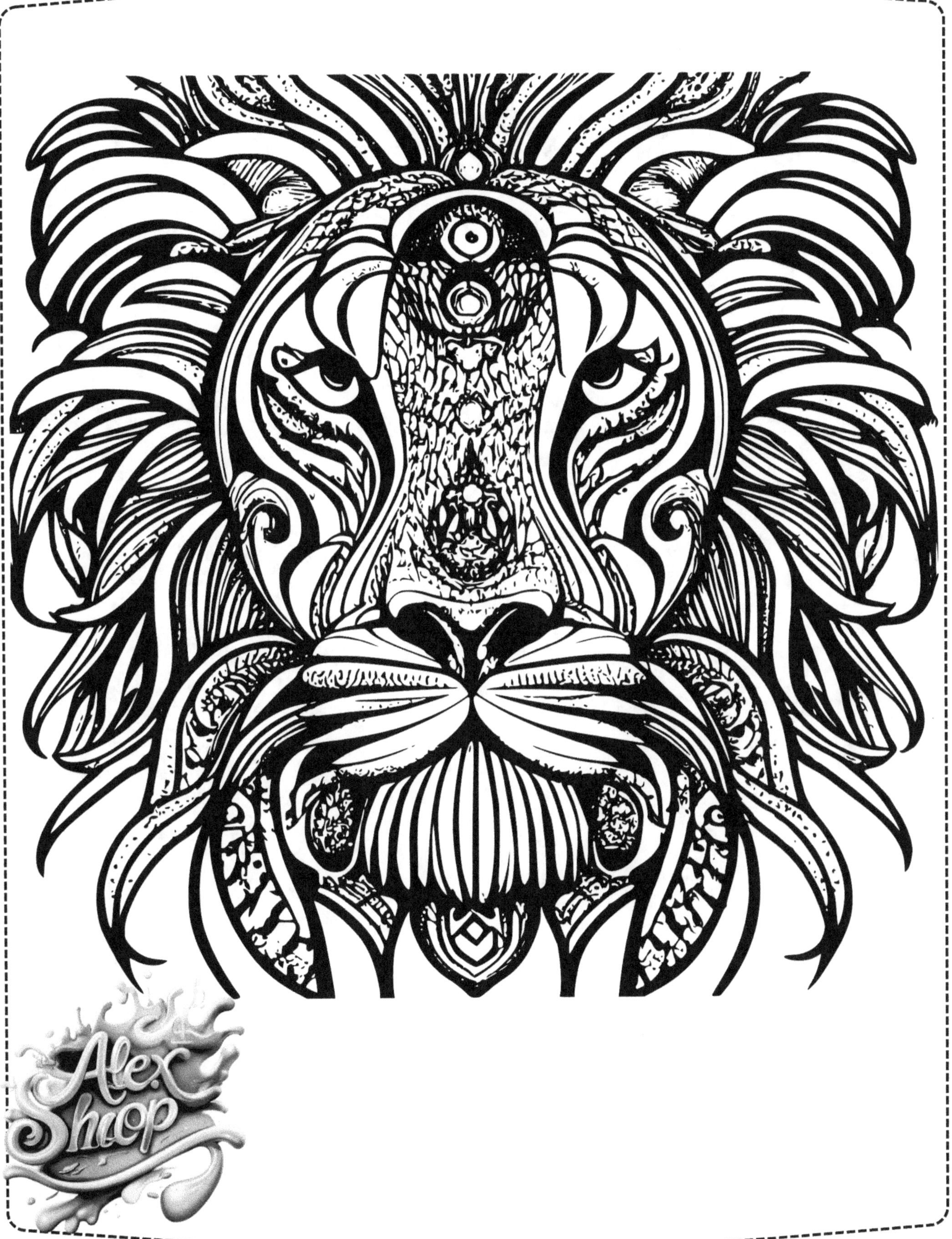
Alex
Shop

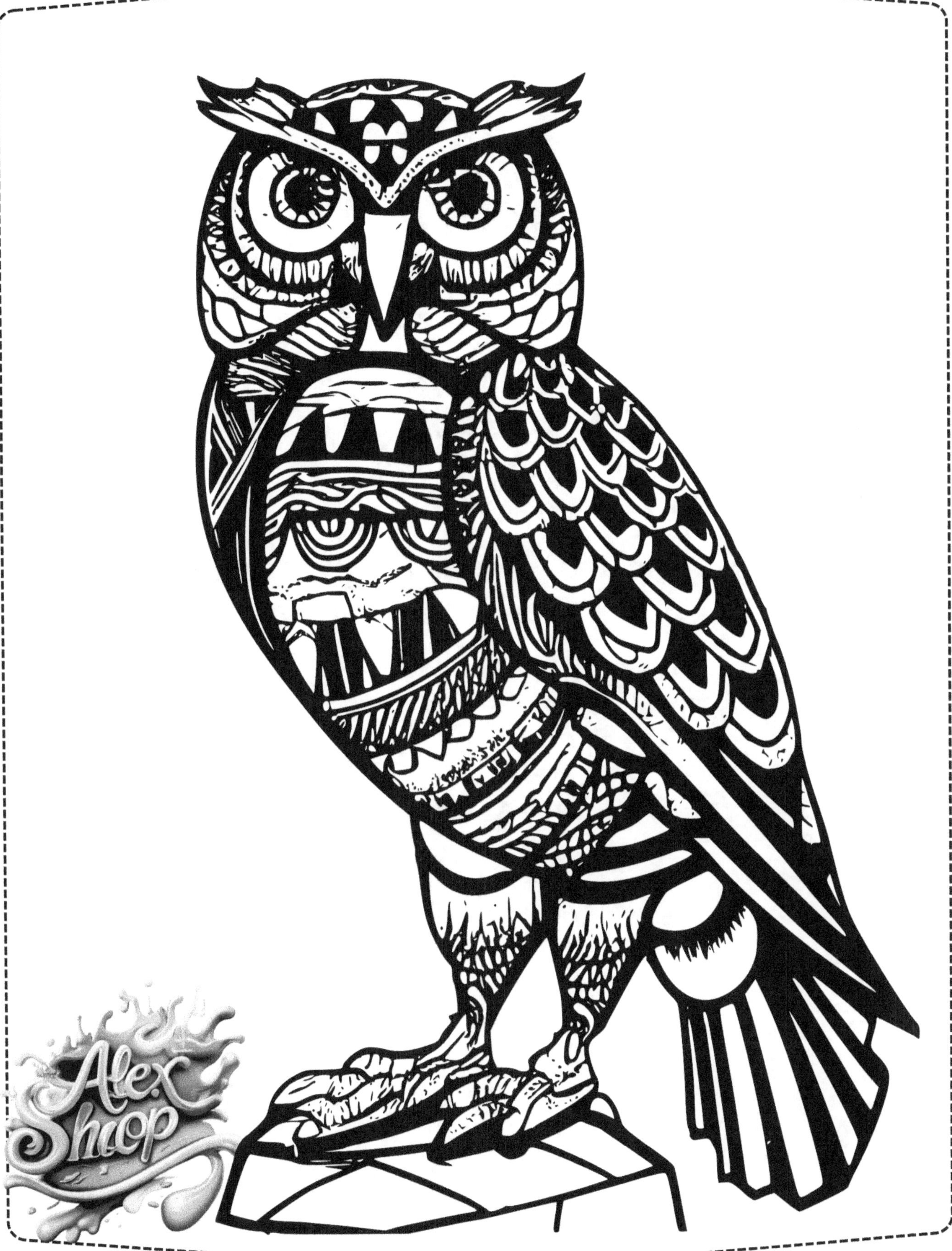
Alex
Shop

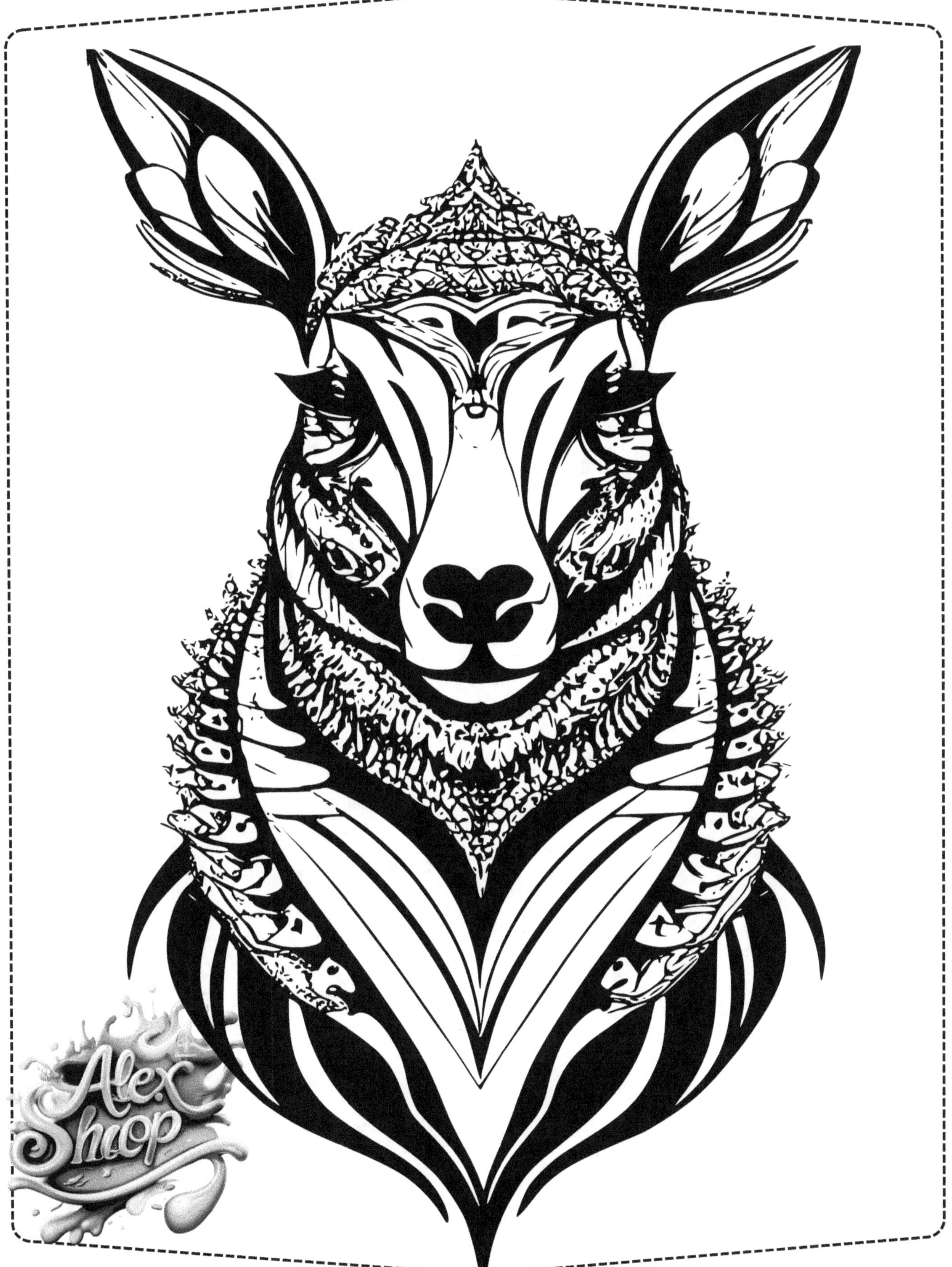
Alex
Shoop